PSH, PTA, and Batman, Oh My!

The Best of *BMC's Film Blog*

(2012-2017)

By Brian Callahan

To Mom, Dad, Shauna and Steve

Table of Contents

"You know who I pray to? Joe Pesci."

-*George Carlin*

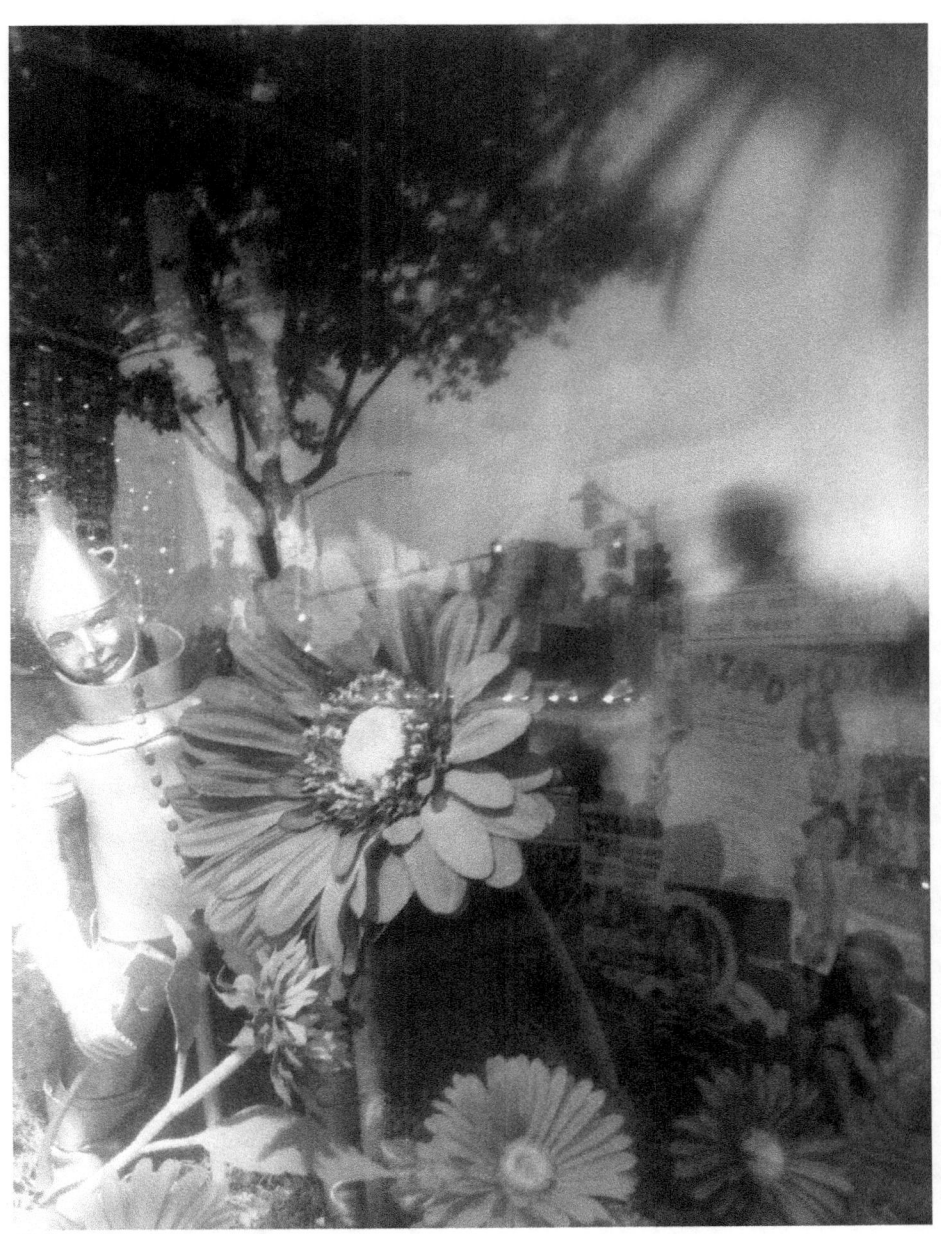

Culver City, Los Angeles

Act I: The Robbery, the Shootout, and the Ridiculously Epic Chase Scene

Int. Bank- Day

The **Dark Knight** Begins

*F*ew movies seem like events nowadays. It's an era where you can stream whatever you want, have thousands of entertainment choices any given night, and are jaded into thinking there's nothing really new anymore, that we are just existing in a recycled vortex of sequels, reboots, and adaptations.

The Dark Knight's opening night was different. I sat next to a dude covered in the Joker's makeup, complete with red scar smile. There were cops in the lobby who were searching people for drugs. My own mental state was concentrated on how Heath Ledger's swan song would unfold. In the audience there was a general stillness, one of those collective experiences where people's consciousnesses are fixed on a single point- mass hypnosis by one of today's master illusionists, Mr. Christopher Nolan.

Whatever haze still lingers as the Warner Brothers logo appears and becomes engulfed in blue flame is cleared as the screen pulls us toward a tall glass building. A violin slowly drones and the reflection of Gotham city in the glass shatters. Thieves grapple into the building and mention someone named the Joker. We see the villain from the back at first, although, because of the mask covering his face and his silence upon entering the vehicle on its way to the bank, it is not yet clear that this is the clown price of crime. As the thieves begin to fall, the money from the vault moves, and the opening notes of the score pick up in their intensity, we begin to see who the Joker is, an agent of chaos who has manipulated his fellow criminals into taking each other down and doing the dirty work of the heist. By the time he pulls off his mask we know it's Ledger's Joker in full-fledged anarchic flesh. He lights a grenade and puts it

in the mouth of the bank's last defender, before he exits stage right
on a bus and the rest of the movie unfolds.

When The Dark Knight Rises opened I speculated on how the
opening scene would live up to the standard set by The Dark Knight.
How can you top a film that was charged by one of the final
outpourings of an actor on the absolute top of his game? A film,
from the opening heist to the closing chase that is as much as you
can hope for in a cinematic experience? With reverence for the past
and tense anticipation for the future, I figured, with memories of
ghosts.

Philip Seymour Hoffman's <u>Capote</u>

To realize Truman Capote on the silver screen is to embody a cauldron of emotions amidst a dance of gesticulations. Philip Seymour Hoffman's performance as the writer is, as he says about the richness of convicted killer Perry Smith's literary potential, "a goldmine."

"Look at how he uses his hands," my uncle once told me about one of Hoffman's more underrated skills as an actor. How Hoffman uses his hands in <u>Capote</u> help show the transformation of the flamboyant toast of the town to the subdued Faustian borrower. These hands, so full of life, twirling with a freewheeling certainty in the first act, go limp by film's end like the tail of a morose cat. They show Capote's nervousness when he is bribing the police chief and tapping his fingers, and his razor-keen focus on the trial proceedings, fingers pressed against his forehead ("his mind is elsewhere," Capote says to Lee at his side, without breaking his hawk-like gaze on Smith).

Other scenes highlight more strengths of Hoffman's acting chops. When Smith[1] tells the story of the murders, Hoffman's eyes rapidly flicker back and forth, as if he is experiencing the rush of excitement Capote would have felt. Not that he thought he was coming close to that level of transmigration, saying in a commentary on the film with director Bennett Miller, "[it's] like when they say about actors, 'they were more that person then that person was,' and I'm like, 'no, not really." He is not merely mimicking Capote, but realizing the person through the dramatic arc of the script and the aesthetic of Miller's film. Sublimely, he takes a footing in this world, applying the "show

---

[1] Poignantly played by Clifton Collins, Jr. Other noteworthy turns here include Catherine Keener as a Harper Lee who goes toe-to-toe with Capote, Bob Balaban as the nebbishy publisher who sort of Satanically eggs Capote on with the book, and Bruce Greenwood, who plays Capote's partner, Jack Dunphy, and reverently conveys how Capote is drifting away and wandering into dangerous territory.

don't tell" adage to the fullest extent. You can see the thoughts whirring inside his head, the moral calculations and their adjoining mental calisthenics moving at full speed until they seem to collapse under the weight of the reality of a situation he can no longer ignore.

As much as he transforms within the film from his state of righteous flamboyance to his moroseness (even the more impressive considering how the scenes were shot out of sequence; the first New York City dinner scene is actually the last shot they made, months after principal photography had concluded), Hoffman made dramatic alterations on his own to step more fully into Capote's shoes. Hoffman began studying the role six months in advance of shooting, reading stories the author wrote, including In Cold Blood and Breakfast at Tiffany's, and listening to recordings of Capote readings from the 1950s, which helped with the scene when he reads excerpts from In Cold Blood in front of a packed auditorium. Whether it's the high-pitched, nasally inflected voice, or the paradoxical toughness of this diminutive man, Hoffman creates a fully rounded character that captures both the spirit of Capote and his role in this story. He adopts Capote's distinct voice wholly into his own being without it being a gimmick, almost as if he's speaking through a perfectly attenuated filter. From a physical standpoint, Hoffman's Capote still feels strong even though he seems small and vulnerable, exemplifying how he tapped into his own persona to find the right notes to play (not to mention that the New York party scenes were all improvised, with one of his monologues inspired by a story from his early days as an actor). It all adds up to an effect of making you feel as if you are not just watching a movie, but peering through a portal into a real man's soul.

Even with all the upfront legwork, Hoffman still struggled over the course of the film with certain parts he thought would have been easier. According to the commentary, several scenes took hours to shoot, with takes going up into the high teens, creating significant frustration on his end that must have challenged his perfectionist workmanship to the brink of its own tolerance. But in working through these difficulties and lingering moments of doubt, he broke through and delivered an effortless performance for the ages. "He's powerless over himself," he says about Capote[2], a statement that may be a reading of Hoffman's own surrendering to the part. It is a rare sort of empathy that can be created when an actor goes to this length, a feeling that takes you out of your own time and space, and into a gray land between the celluloid and your mind, as open and expansive as the lonesome fields of Kansas in winter, and as chilling as the crime conveyed by the title of Capote's magnum opus.

~~~

---

[2] Also in the commentary, which is available on the original DVD.

Retaking the <u>Road to Perdition</u>

Back in the summer of 2002, I was set to go to my first concert with my brother, Steve. Soon after we pulled off the highway onto the main drag on the way to the Tweeter Center in Mansfield, MA, we got the message – Lenny Kravitz, soon to be forever coronated by us as "Princess Lenny," had to cancel the show due to an unfortunate case of sore throat. Faced with the prospect of lamely going home, we decided on seeing *Road to Perdition* for a second time, which I recall being a relatively easy decision at the time for us and one I'm still glad we made 14 years later, as it has remained one of my favorite movies.

I watched *Road to Perdition* again recently and enjoyed seeing how it still holds up. The performances of the ensemble cast still give me chills, especially Tom Hanks in a rare turn as the antihero, Jude Law as the creepy assassin Maguire, and Paul Newman as the fading, ruthless mobster patriarch. Newman plays John Rooney, who leads an Irish organized crime ring in a small Midwestern town in the early twentieth century. Rooney's God-like control over his dominion belies a weakness for a traitorous son, Connor, played with just the right amount of spinelessness and guile by Daniel Craig.

These performances are captured by the Oscar-winning cinematography of the late Conrad L. Hall, who also shot *American Beauty, Butch Cassidy and the Sundance Kid*, and *Cool Hand Luke*, among others, and whose framing, lighting, and perspective throughout the film give the story an epic, timeless quality that evokes the biblical place identified in the title. A few of his cinematic compositions always stand out to me, viewing after viewing: the perspective flattening zoom-in as Maguire walks into the scene, the view from the hole in the warehouse showing us how Michael Sullivan Jr. (Tyler Hoechlin[3]) is watching an event that will re-shape his view of his father, the close-up on the hands of John

---

[3] Who, fourteen years later, plays the baseball ax-chopping McReynolds in <u>Everybody Wants Some!!</u>

Rooney and Michael Sullivan playing a haunting piano duet, the shootout in the darkened rainy alleyway, lit by streetlights and gunfire, a closing bathroom door showing us a mirror reflecting the dead body of Connor Rooney in the bathtub. Not only do these shots show you the action of the scene in a riveting manner that takes full advantage of the cinematic canvas, they are able to convey a deeper, resonant message – a villain who blurs the perspective of his day job and his true evils, a young adult looking up from a narrow point of view who is unable to fully process what he is seeing, two hands from two different people with two different positions who are walking the same line and playing the same song, the moving reflection of the real thing as film itself, and, okay, the shootout in the rain is just damn cool.

Not to mention the deft use of sound, the waves rolling back and forth as Mike Sullivan's bullet-ridden, blood-soaked body slides down a window pane, Thomas Newman's haunting score used to evoke a variety of moods – the nostalgia of a bygone era, the grandeur of Chicago in the 1930s, the tension of watching Alexander Rance (Dylan Baker) stall Mike Sullivan as Maguire makes his way into their room.

As orchestrated by Sam Mendes, who would go on to work with Craig in two James Bond movies (who would have guessed Craig's sniveling, thin-skinned character would be a precursor role to 007?), these elements come together in a way that makes the story of a man who righteously fights his way to hell, and lets his son find salvation in the process (adapted by David Self from the graphic novel by Max Allen Collins and Richard Piers Rayner), one that opened up my mind of what film could do. It wasn't one of those AFI Top 100 films that felt bestowed upon me by critics of a bygone age, something I felt like I had to like, but rather something I could love pretty easily, and am glad to have begun re-watching all those years back.

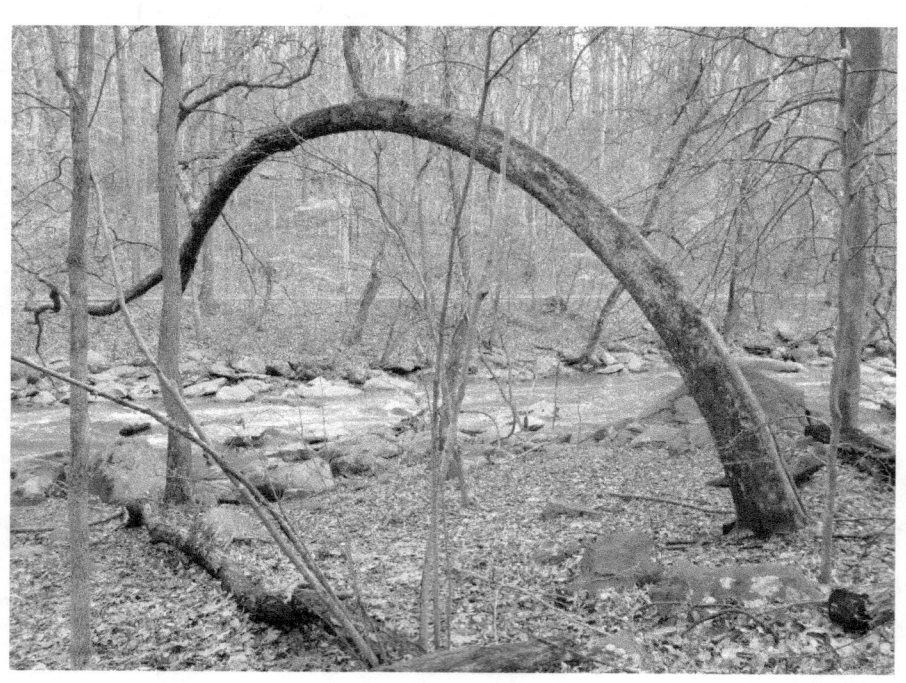

Rock Creek Park, Washington, D.C.

Bourne, Revisited (<u>The Bourne Identity</u> Series)

Probably the main question surrounding the 2012 reboot of the Bourne franchise, with Jeremy Renner, is how do you continue the series, or attempt to reinvent it, without the Jason Bourne we know played by Matt Damon? To prepare myself for <u>The Bourne Legacy</u>, I went back and watched the three Damon films that preceded it. Over the course of this trilogy, Jason Bourne moves in a sort of paradox, his trip forward in space triggers memories that move him backward through time. He realizes he is responsible for the evil that has become bound to his life, despite his best efforts to fight it head on. Bourne's rebellion is righteous, even if he had a hand in creating the conditions that were necessary for it to arise in the first place. I liken him to a sort of modern Man with No Name from Sergio Leone's excellent <u>Fistful of Dollars</u> trilogy (these films even bear a similarity to the Bourne ones, at least in the thematic structure, because the links between the movies are more of a character's overall journey rather than an overlapping plot like <u>Star Wars</u>). Finding out his true name over the course of the series does not make Bourne any less of a mystery. What led him to the Treadstone lab in the first place? Where was the Man with No Name wandering from? Where does fighting lead? How do you move forward when you carry the heavy burden of a past that cannot be undone?[4]

Here are a few other notes I have on the Bourne films:

---

[4] **Editor's Note**: In the 2016 <u>Jason Bourne</u>, which basically just smacked down <u>The Bourne Legacy</u> into a crumpled pit of meaninglessness, some of these questions are answered – Jason Bourne is led into the Treadstone program by his dad, Richard Webb, because, you know, he's actually David Webb. Richard Webb realizes the program is actually a sinister assassination squad so he pulls his son out of the program, only to get offed himself. From there, Jason Bourne stays in the program, kills a target, then awakens on a boat and begins to understand the true nature of things. Fighting and a series of espionage-type maneuvers help him figure out what's going on, which usually involves a shady CIA director and more secrets about the Treadstone program. He could presumably stop kicking ass and figuring things out, resigning himself to a life in the shadows, but then, where would the fun in that be?

- There are some truly great blank face expressions from Matt Damon throughout this series, especially when he talks with women. The best is when Julia Stiles' character alludes to a tryst the two had that Bourne has no recollection of whatsoever. I could not tell whether Bourne actually did not remember or if he was playing dumb because he did not want to risk her life like he did with Marie (Franka Potente). It is part of a great performance overall by Damon. He is understated throughout the films yet you can feel the intense pulse of his character as he goes in and out of trouble.
- Potente's early death in <u>The Bourne Supremacy</u> is still a major bummer years after seeing it for the first time. She is so good in her role, holding her own as the female action star counterpart to Damon, and so undeniably magnetic, that when you know she's gone you wonder how the films will replace her. Stiles and Joan Allen provide solid performances but they are not nearly electric as Potente.
- With <u>The Bourne Ultimatum</u>, David Strathairn pulls off an impressive/random trifecta of cool movie roles: as the overzealous CIA lead here, the legendary television reporter Edward R. Murrow in <u>Good Night, and Good Luck</u>, and, of course, the dude who gets eaten by a T-Rex while taking a dump in <u>Jurassic Park</u>.

Notes from Hell's Kitchen: The Man Without Fear? (Daredevil)

One of my favorite parts of the second season of *Daredevil* is when newspaper editor Mitchell Ellison (Geoffrey Cantor) leads Karen Page (Deborah Ann Woll) into the former office of the late reporter Ben Urich (Vondie Curtis-Hall), who was last seen murdered by the very subject of his exposé, taking the story with him to the grave. She knows the implications of the gesture and so do we. She is not really an over-worked, under-paid legal assistant at Nelson and Murdock, she is a true-blue hound of an investigative reporter, taking Urich's torch and running with it. It is an unsurprising surprise that works within the contours of the story we know, yet alters the narrative's course in a way that keeps you engaged with the material and excited for what comes next.

These types of changes worked particularly well in the second season of the show, as one of its major challenges heading in was how to top what was an exceptionally well-executed superhero origin story as told in a serialized television format. How do you continue doing the things that made this show the exciting, larger-than-life mythic adventure tale that it is, while breaking new ground, providing the audience something that is self-contained, and still leaving the door open for continued storylines? For the supporting characters like Page and her onetime colleague Foggy Nelson (Elden Henson), it helps to throw challenges in their paths and see how they approach these situations.

For Page, Nelson, and that other colleague of theirs, Matt Murdock (Charlie Cox) also known as the Devil of Hell's Kitchen, or more simply, Daredevil, this challenge comes in the form of a man named Frank Castle, who goes by the apt moniker, the Punisher. As played by Jon Bernthal[5], the Punisher comes onto the scene as a one-man force of destructive nature, a Marine veteran who is out to kill a cadre of criminals involved in the murder of his family, and who will go to all lengths to complete his mission. It is clear early on that

---

[5] Who has also done good work in *The Walking Dead* and *The Accountant*.

Hell's Kitchen is a chaotic warzone, with no sanctuaries to be found, not even in the church, which is the site of a massacre that occurs early in the first episode.

Having the Punisher as the antagonizing force for the show on the heels of the Kingpin (Vincent D'Onofrio) was an inspired choice, as it changed the game from being about the defeat of another villain to a battle of philosophies on heroism, law, justice, order, and chaos. Although Daredevil seemed to be on the side of virtue, he found an opponent fighting for a similar end, just with a starkly different, murderous approach. In a key conversation in episode three, Daredevil and the Punisher debate the merits of their actions and try to convince the other to change, both thinking the differences in how they go about their business justifies the very activities that are questionable in the first place.

When the Punisher is arrested in the fourth episode you wonder where exactly the season will go, as it seems that he has been set up to be the main antagonist for the season, especially with Wilson Fisk in the big box. You soon realize, though, as the trial of the Punisher gets underway, the trial of the century as deemed by the show's main players, that this has all been prologue for the real meat of the season. The firm of Nelson and Murdock defends the seemingly indefensible Castle in this trial, providing an opportunity for Nelson to shine on a big stage, for Page to follow her acute sense that there is more to the man with the hole in his skull, and for Murdock to fall from grace in this public sphere, as the demons he faces in his private arena multiply considerably.

To be fair, it doesn't help the man with the super-powered senses that maybe the craziest of all possible ex-lovers shows up back in his life, a prodigious ninja assassin known as Elektra (played with delicious, scenery chewing glee by Elodie Yung). Her backstory is told in a manner similar to how she is introduced in the Frank Miller Daredevil origin story, *The Man Without Fear*, as a free-spirited society woman who corrupts Murdock as a younger, law student[6].

---

[6] Although from what I recall about the comic, the television adaptation paints the nature of the Elektra/Murdock separation more starkly, as a matter of significant

After a brief fling that climaxes in a knife party of sorts, they depart in, oh let's just say, not the most amicable of ways.

Fast forward to the present timeline. Murdock has his life going pretty well at the moment, something seems to be brewing with Karen, and the chance to represent the Punisher in court could be the big break his fledgling law firm needs. The last thing he needs at this juncture is to go back down a path he wisely averted, but Elektra starts contacting him and, resist as he tries, he is pulled back into her world. Soon Daredevil and Elektra are battling The Hand, the invisible army of a seemingly immortal ninja named Nobu (Peter Shinkoda), and staring down the abyss into bottomless pits. The partnership between Elektra and Daredevil is an alliance that rests on the slipperiest of slopes, and is impacted by subsequent discoveries about the true natures of their motives in completing this mission and operating in an ever-darkening world.

This fight against The Hand becomes the final dramatic arc in the second season that ends without the complete resolution that made the first season so satisfying. Just as we think the season may end, with Daredevil mourning the loss of Elektra on the rooftop, we are presented with snippets of What is Coming. But while Elektra may come back to life, Kingpin may return, and Frank may be even worse than he was before, these seem tangential to the arc we see in the show's titular protagonist as he dives further away from reality into the vigilante abyss: has Daredevil defeated not only the obvious villains, but Matthew Murdock himself?

---

ethical differences rather than someone who was literally too much too handle. Given the television Murdock's strong initial resistance at Elektra's re-entry into his life, I thought they may have been better served by leaving this backstory out, or giving it a few more examples to really drive home the rationale for Murdock's lingering disgust. It was one of the few clunky parts I noticed this season, but whaddaya do?

Zombie Movies in 2013 (<u>World War Z</u> and <u>Warm Bodies</u>)

That there is not much similarity between <u>Warm Bodies</u> and <u>World War Z</u> is a testament to the spectrum of stories you can tell on the zombie palette (pre-blood smear at least). You can have a zomedy, zom-com, or one where you hope they just eat everyone and put the audience out of its misery. Even though George A. Romero deserves his due as the genre's auteur, I welcome the different takes of the modern age for being both enjoyable and thought provoking.

<u>World War Z</u> is <u>Jurassic Park</u>-esque in how it exists in a sinister world where danger lurks around every corner. Many films falter on having too much action and not enough breathing room, but <u>World War Z</u> somehow managed to have a ton of thrilling sequences and run a meaningful dramatic course. Maybe evoking Moses in the end is ridiculous, but, hey, when you part a zombie sea you gotta give credit where credit's due.

In <u>Warm Bodies</u>, there is a flickering remnant of humanity that lets the protagonist, simply named R, dream. What does this zombie see in Julie, even before he takes Dave Franco's brains, that makes him regain what he has lost? Is R human in the end because he changed into one or was he always slightly human all along? How much zombie remains? How do we define zombieness? How much zombie are we? Similar to how Romero used his zombie films for a societal commentary on consumerist culture, Jonathan Levine has his <u>Warm Bodies</u> pose a new set of questions for our digital age, and in asking how much humanity is in a zombie, makes us ask how much zombie is in ourselves?

Does Robert Englund Dream of Electric Krueger Kruller Kool Aid Acid?

Here are some notes from the horror/Halloween films I watched in October 2016:

The Conjuring – I rented this 2013 film starring Vera Farmiga (*Up in the Air*) and Patrick Wilson (*Fargo*) from the video store in my apartment building, which seems about right. This movie is part of the *Exorcism* class of horror films, with a bit of paranormal investigation blended in. At first I thought it was going to be more of a haunted doll-type film, which I particularly enjoy, but it turns out the doll is just the vessel for a greater type of evil spirit lurking upon the haunted grounds of the house a poor family moves into. Beyond a creepy musical instrument that reflects ghosts in the background when it is played, I wasn't particularly scared during this, but *The Conjuring* was enjoyable for the most part.

Abbott and Costello Meet Dr. Jekyll and Mr. Hyde – The Abbott and Costello movies still hold up surprisingly well, they are filled with clever one-liners and slapstick that wouldn't be too out of place in a Will Ferrell movie. I also really enjoy the aesthetic- black and white, with classic movie set production stages, cameos from Universal monsters (in this one Lou Costello goes into a wax museum in London and stumbles across a briefly awoken Frankenstein and others), and smoothly conjured set pieces that help the films move at a brisk, enjoyable pace.

The Wicker Man – There are movies that make you revel at the power of the cinema, that make you appreciate being alive in a myriad of new ways, that make you marvel at the capacity for human achievement, and maybe make you reach for the stars in your own right. The Nicolas Cage version of *The Wicker Man* is not one of those films. But for those who enjoy their bad Cage movies like a bottle of nice wine, think of *The Wicker Man* as a signature vintage, but be careful, it will give you a strong case of delirium and may make you go slightly insane yourself.

Leprechaun: Origins – After days of reeling from *The Wicker Man*, I made my triumphant return to the land of Serious cinema with *Leprechaun: Origins*, a WWE Studios-produced movie that was the first Leprechaun movie since 2003's *Leprechaun Back 2 tha Hood*. I remember seeing this at a going-out-of-business FYE sale and being surprised a new Leprechaun movie had escaped my notice, only to realize it did not star the great Warwick Davis, but some wrestler more commonly known by his moniker Hornswoggle. Without Davis, and by attempting a more serious, slasher-type approach to the story, this Leprechaun story was pretty dull (although it did have some solid make-up that gave its monster a retro, Swamp Thing-type look). Where's me pot of Davis? Where indeed.

Cabin in the Woods – This 2011 film features just about all you could ask for from a Halloween flick – a solid ensemble cast featuring Chris Hemsworth, Sigourney Weaver, Richard Jenkins, and the great Bradley Whitford; a creative premise that subverts horror tropes; just the right amount of camp to keep things light without devolving into *Bride of Chucky* territory; some social commentary that's not thrown in your face; some awesome unintentional comedy (I'll see your Samuel L. Jackson death scene and raise you a Chris Hemsworth); a ridiculous, over-the-top third act; and monsters galore. My one problem was that it's not really that scary. I don't think it was necessarily aiming to be scary, but then again, why not be?

Nightmare on Elm Street – Needing something to address my dearth of horrification here (I'm not averse to truly scary films but sometimes feel like I'm just putting a pinky toe into the water with this world), I finally checked off this classic from horror master Wes Craven. In some ways I felt as if I had seen this film already, and half-expected Groundskeeper Willie to show up at some point. This *Simpsons* foregrounding kept me from falling into the abyss, but it is a pretty frightening premise that does have some truth in the if-you-die-while-you're-sleeping-then-you're-really-dead urban legend, and the Johnny Depp death scene may be even more enjoyable than the *Cabin in the Woods* Chris Hemsworth one, given Depp's own descent into despicableness. Thinking of Depp in the real world also made me wonder about Robert Englund and how he must be a well-adjusted dude if he's able to continue to play this guy across his career (Jack Nicholson says the Joker, for one, is a hard character to get out of his head. Does Robert Englund then have Krueger residue lingering in his subconscious? Can he even dream of his own manifestation without creating a paradoxical riff that causes this world to collapse on itself before it even begins?).

Jeepers Creepers – My attorney recommended this to me when I mentioned I was thinking of seeing *Nightmare on Elm Street*, citing it as having some similarities to the classic slasher flick. To me, one of the main ways the films overlap is how one of the characters dreams in advance about the grisly murders committed by a bogeyman-type monster. The way the monster physically dominates his victims whenever he is in enclosed spaces with them, how you get the sense he is on a never-ending rampage, even when out of the frame, is another. This is an early film role (2001!) for Justin Long, who is also in *Drag Me to Hell* if you are looking for another heartwarming tear-jerker this Halloween season.

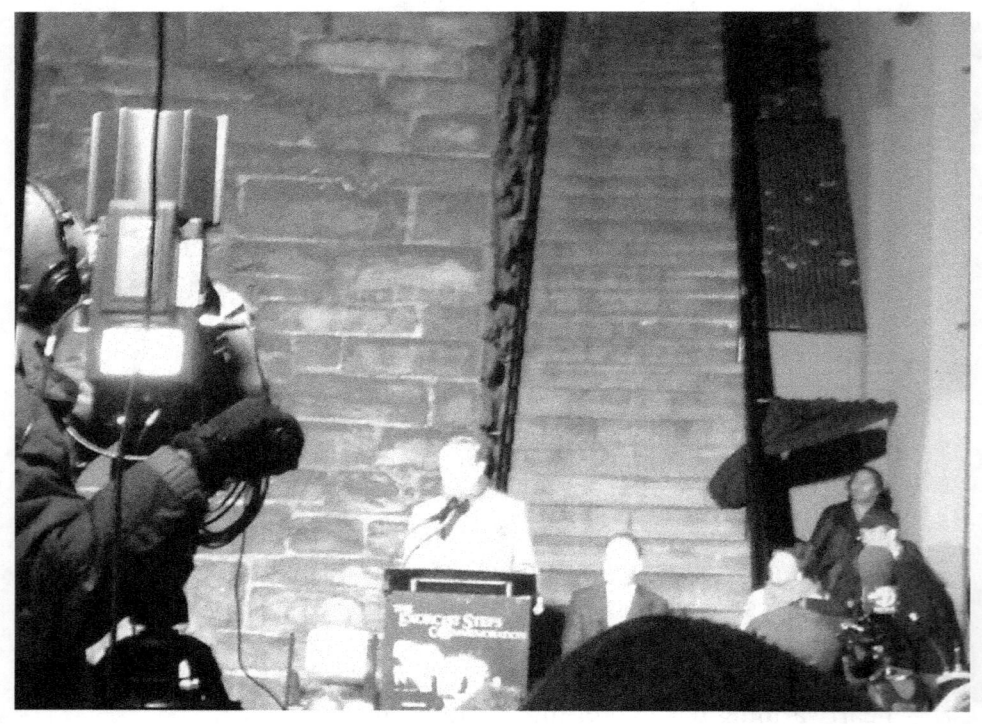

Legendary filmmaker William Friedkin, alongside The Exorcist author William Peter Blatty and mayor Muriel Bowser, at the dedication of The Exorcist steps in Georgetown, Washington, D.C.

Classic Film? <u>The Curse of Chucky</u>

Still yearning for a healthy dose of Halloween movie cheesiness in the wake of *Leprechaun: Origins*, I went to the only other place I could go besides the Leprechaun's emerald, salty-barb-filled domain – to the land of Chucky. Directed again by Rob Mancini, who has admirably helmed all of the Chucky movies, and starring Brad Dourif (as opposed to some C-list WWEer), along with his granddaughter, Fiona Dourif, *The Curse of Chucky* marks a triumphant return to the franchise's earlier darker tone yet still retains an adequate level of camp and absurdity that only a movie with an ugly homicidal doll can provide.

Early on in the film, a strange package arrives at the house of the poor family set to be traumatized, comprised for the time being of wheelchair-bound Nica (as played by Fiona Dourif) and her mother. The package contains our titular villain (I was going to say anti-hero, but it's hard to call a serial killer a hero of any sort, even though you kind of root for him to kill the annoying people in the movie), and soon, all hell breaks loose. The mother's unexplainable murder in the night triggers the arrival of the rest of the family, who are relatively Tolstoy-esque in the familial dysfunction they bring to the table (old Leo just rolled over in his frosty Russian grave). For the family's first dinner together, we see them have a delicious looking chili that comes with one serious problem- it's laced with a little pepper-crusted poison by you know who. For some reason, the poison only affects the priest, the only one you'd think karma should favor in this situation, so he leaves, wrecks his car, and gets decapitated. It takes a while for anyone to guess anything is wrong, although I know if I were there, I'd immediately suspect the doll and kick him in the face.

The rest of this aforementioned evening is filled with what you'd expect – grisly electrocutions, stabbings, axe-beheadings – presented in some clever ways that still keep you on your tippy toes, like when Nica's brother-in-law suspects his wife is cheating on him with the au pair, so he installs a mini-camera in Chucky to nab her in the act, only to ultimately see the horrors of everything that has happened so far unfold, with the live recording of it all actually somehow appearing to be walking behind him, and cackling.

The ending of it all is a little drawn out and *Return of the King*-y, complete with a somewhat convoluted but artfully shot flashback sequence showing Chucky in human Brad Dourif form, and seems like it's serving as set-up for more installments, but I thought it was smart to have Nica save the day only to be framed for the murders and come off as insane in the trial proceedings. I hope we see more of Fiona Dourif after this and in different types of roles, as she definitely shows the capacity to play people who are strong-willed, slightly-off-the-rails, and righteously heroic. Until then, let us pay respect to our favorite doll from hell, even if that means slightly misplaced, reverent appeasement for wickedly unsurprising deeds, lest he arrive in a package on our doorsteps, and we forget who he is.

Stepping into **Jurassic World**

On the road to Jurassic World, I was as skeptical as any that the film would happen, and would actually be any good once it saw the light of day. I still feel the pang of disappointment over Jurassic Park III, which is the easily the most let down I have ever felt with a movie, worse than watching Shia Lebeouf in the fourth Indiana Jones, worse than singing Tobey Maguire in Spider-Man 3, worse than the teeny bopper fest of the sixth Harry Potter. And rumors over the years did nothing to disquiet my sadness over this once mighty series, marked by grand master Steven Spielberg's iconic original, and his underrated follow-up. There was talk of a whole movie being built around the premise of a velociraptor army, which, although it figures into this movie as the dark motive of the Vincent D'onofrio character, would have been better served as a SyFy movie. Rebooting and reimagining Jurassic Park then seemed akin to the task facing BD Wong[7] in the original film, how do you bring an extinct species roaring back to life?

New franchise steward Colin Trevorrow did an admirable job in this endeavor, even though he does fall prey to the temptations inherent in making a reboot. Unlike Joe Johnston, the Jurassic Park III director, who, if memory serves me correctly, dished up one dinosaur chase after another in a non-step dino-rama, devoid of any suspense, fear, or fun, Trevorrow pays fitting homage to Spielberg and other monster mavens of the past, and injects his own style onto the proceedings. Trevorrow uses his talents here to render the ferocious colossus that is the Indominus Rex, a super-charged t-rex that is like Godzilla after too many cups of coffee. This iRex is the catalyst for the mayhem, which features, among other things, a carnivorous-pterodactyl reenactment of Hitchcock's The Birds, the carnage of a sea serpent monster seemingly out of Pacific Rim, and a

---

[7] Who is back here in Jurassic World. Also look out for the DNA cartoon guy, the night-vision goggles Tim and Lex use to see the T-Rex in the rain, the Jurassic Park jeeps, and Ingen equipment from The Lost World. And is that the Dilophosaurus flashing as one of the holograms in the Jurassic World visitor's center?

raptor, motorcycle chase that reminds me of similar scenes in The Wizard of Oz and The Return of the Jedi.

Much like the imperfection wrought in the new breed of rex, there are still some things left to be desired here. For me, this begins and ends with the homo sapiens sapiens. There are some efforts to ground the story through the arcs of the characters, namely how the bond between Gray and Zach strengthens over their parents impending divorce, and the romance between Chris Pratt's raptor wrangler and Bryce Dallas Howard's businesswoman (who somehow makes it through the whole film in high heels[8]), not to mention the greed at play in Vincent D'Onofrio's[9] raptor army ambitions. However, these still seem secondary to the mechanics of the greater need to get as many awesome dinos in the movie as possible, which may be a dark portent for franchise's future[10].

Even though its immediate and potential commercial success may overshadow its inherent artistic merit, I think there is something in Jurassic World worth savoring, at least for the present moment. For me, it rekindled memories of visiting Disney World and watching The Lost World in the theaters with my Mom. And I imagine there will be a similar feeling on successive viewings, especially when John Williams' goddamned perfect score begins its triumphant march into the happy stores of my brain. The nearby reptilian quadrant of my cranium may take some carnal delight at this repetition into delirium, relishing this movie as theme park, and sensing some sweet morsel at the edge of its purview, or at least some encounters with its closely related ancestors. But I will not think about this, just feel as if I can enter this sublime, subtropical, ancient world anew, even though I have been there before.

---

[8] My other beef is with the egregious lack of any Jurassic World Disaster Recovery plan. You're telling me you don't have a bunker there after everything that has happened in this fictional world?

[9] Whose strong character acting here came fresh off the heels of his excellent performance as Wilson Fisk in season 1 of Daredevil.

[10] I know I'm saying this after the fourth movie in a series that has yielded so much money it probably has like the 14th highest GDP in the world, but still.

Dawn of the Planet of the Apes

Although I am generally at odds with what seems an increasing over-reliance on special effects in big budget movies, I thought Matt Reeves' film skillfully used envelope-pushing technology in telling its story of how genetically-enhanced apes, immune to a virus that wipes out most of the earth's human population, irrevocably seized power and firmly established a new era of rule. As much as I like to go to the movies to be challenged and think differently, at the end of the day I go to be entertained, and no film succeeded at that more for me than this one, from the thrilling jungle hunt in the beginning, to how the apes on horseback scene is perfectly set to a pounding, percussion-laden score, and through the climactic fight on the scaffolding between Ceasar and Koba. If we are subject to more and more over-the-top special effects in the years to come, I can only hope the technology is as expertly used as it is here, anchored in Andy Serkis' motion-capture brilliance and realized in a new world order hurtling toward an epoch we can only imagine[11].

---

[11] See bmclassahan.tumblr.com for my take on *War for the Planet of the Apes*.

2001 on Steroids? (<u>Prometheus</u>)

When I heard the Ridley Scott quotation that <u>Prometheus</u> was "2001 on steroids" I was immediately jacked up. <u>2001: A Space Odyssey</u> is one of the coolest mind-benders I have ever seen and if this new film did follow through on Scott's proclamation then we would have been in for a serious treat. <u>Prometheus </u>definitely has a neo-<u>2001</u> vibe to it, from the finger-nail earth opening shot homage to the android David. But how much does it capture the essence of Stanley Kubrick's classic?

Both films start out on earth, although the beginning in <u>2001</u> is more startling and provides the viewer a symbolic image (the monolith) and foundational behavior (chaotic, animal fighting) as frames to understand the film. <u>Prometheus</u>' opening is somewhat more muddled, giving us a <u>Gravity</u>-esque panorama of earth and a scene in which an engineer drinks some black goo and dies.

To get a sense of the narrative progression, follow the ships. <u>Prometheus</u> spends much of its time documenting a cave expedition. The ship lands on the planet, the crew explores a pertinent cave region, controversy is stirred between different team members with different agendas (essentially entrepreneurial versus scientific), aliens attack and latch onto and into explorers, aliens interbreed, and a back-up ship escapes. In <u>2001</u>, the ship finds a mysterious substance on the moon and departs into space, where it stays and goes through vortices, light fields, and other galactic formations. In short, when the Prometheus ship is grounded, which is the bulk of the film, the possibilities of the plot become static as well. Since <u>2001</u> keeps moving you never know where it is going to go even after the end, imparting a thrilling, exploratory sensation that gives the film considerable power.

As they travel into and out of these places, the characters are shaped by the interactions they have with their robots. In <u>2001</u> the flight

34

crew travels with a supercomputer named HAL 9000. The Prometheus crew goes with a humanoid cyborg named David. These powerful machines represent the progress of science to the point that humans can be creators. Our capability to make artificial life creates a sort of God-complex that helps decipher the human motivations at play in these stories. The 2001 crew thinks that HAL 9000 can be controlled and has limits because of its artificial nature. HAL 9000 thinks more in terms of how to make the humans subservient to the mission, creating a rift that necessitates the termination of one of the parties. In Prometheus, David wants to understand Peter Weyland by supporting the Weyland Industry's mission of discovering the true nature of our origins[12]. To achieve his goal, David must use the human knowledge he has acquired to communicate with a type of alien we will come to know as an engineer[13], which ends up ripping his head off. This idea of creation is bonded with the idea of destruction. In 2001 the machine that should be helping the astronauts turns on them. In Prometheus the machine is more helpful, but is ultimately kind of useless[14].

Perhaps no cinematic element embodies the "2001 on steroids" proclamation, however, as much as the differences in the casts. Prometheus is more of an ensemble than 2001, which is essentially driven by two actors and a voice. The personification of David reflects this key difference. Michael Fassbender is excellent as David in a role he was literally born to play because we all know he was genetically created in a German lab to act (and if he wasn't I mean, seriously, he has to make an emotionless character compelling and conform to specific programmed functions that are interwoven into his artificial DNA?). Noomi Rapace also delivers as Dr. Elizabeth Shaw. She is both the tough Sigourney Weaver Ripley, who is able to rip out an alien from her stomach, and a heartfelt lover and explorer, who feels pain from her inability to bear children, yet still feels hope from the incredibly pioneering position she is in. And

---

[12] Weyland's dying wish basically.

[13] An ancient species with the power to create life that also lacks much of a sense of humor, or maybe just has a very dark one.

[14] "I see your comment and raise you an Alien: Covenant," says Ridley Scott upon reading this.

Idris Elba is fun to watch as the tough, practical, brave, and lady-killing ship captain Janek. On the other hand, more is not always better. Some of the characters are cardboard soldiers who are there to be alien fodder. Charlize Theron is somewhat wasted as one-note Weyland heir Meredith Vickers. And there is Guy Pearce, who plays an old man despite being a relatively young man in real life. Sometimes focusing in on a few characters amplifies the emotions of those people (as in Gravity, Cast Away, or 127 Hours), which gives 2001 an edge, because it concentrates the plot on a few characters, amplifying the emotions of their conflict, not to mention the dramatic stakes of their situation.

Despite their differences, a commonality between the stories is in their gorgeous direction. The opening of Prometheus rivals anything out of Planet Earth, and there are sequences throughout that gave me the proverbial goosebumps, such as David's visualization of the engineering process, the rock storm, Shaw's Caesarean section, and the images of holographic engineers running through the cave tunnels. In 2001, Kubrick's groundbreaking work still more than holds up today. The choreography of his camera-work to the score and movements of his actors is textbook cinematic excellence. One of the more striking examples is how he uses the classical song "Blue Danube" as you go out of the dawn of humankind to space, from proto-human bone to human-engineered spacecraft. Scott counters in Prometheus by using Chopin's "Prelude for Piano No. 15 in D Flat Major, Op. 28 No. 15" as a way to introduce us to David's superhuman intelligence. Both songs amplify the action of their respective sequences and leave a lasting imprint on the imagination.

In the end, Dr. Shaw declares the Prometheus ship to be "still searching." While we found the answer to the genesis of the creature in the Alien films there are still some unanswered questions from Prometheus that simultaneously make it a frustrating yet tantalizing experience. How was the black goo created? Why wouldn't our engineers even talk to us? Who created the engineers (or is this question essentially a way of saying our questions are other species' and aliens' questions as well?)?

Steroids may help you hit a baseball farther or do feats beyond the range of normal human capability. Space travel may someday take us beyond the borders of our solar system into lands that we could never have imagined. In many ways though, we have the tools to achieve these feats without the need of artificial enhancement or engineering marvels. Prometheus may go far and represent the spectacular possibilities of story-telling in the computer-generated century, but it is also a reminder that the most powerful mysteries are still left as open cases in the dark of space, where the only sound you can hear is the silence of souls vanquished by aliens, and robots.

Bojack Horseman- "Fish Out of Water"

While watching "Fish Out of Water", the fourth episode of the third season of the *Netflix* animated series *Bojack Horseman*, I realized I was watching something that was pretty extraordinary. As much as I love the series when it plays its usual off-kilter, black comedy, surreal, avant garde anthropomorphic universe notes, this was something that seemed to go into another world. This was true not only in terms of its literal setting, an underwater city in the Pacific Ocean that felt like the Water Temple in *The Legend of Zelda: Ocarina of Time*, Sofia Coppola's Tokyo in *Lost in Translation*, the underwater settings of *Finding Nemo* and *Finding Dory*, and, of course, Bikini Bottom in *Spongebob Squarepants*, but in the essentially silent film mode in which the episode was told. Only in the beginning and end of the episode do you hear any spoken dialogue, besides the burbles and gurgles spoken with accompanying bubbles by all the characters, as well as a few handwritten notes that chronicle Bojack's struggle in reconnecting with the former director of the movie he is now promoting. If "Fish Out of Water" were merely about his trials and tribulations in meeting up with a person from the past he feels he's wronged it would be enough, but this being *Bojack Horseman*, it throws in a plot thread about a male seahorse giving birth on a bus and having Bojack help one of the lost seahorse babies get back to its father, somehow showing us the decency and pain of a character who we have known to be a fallen exemplar of excess, who is filled with self-loathing and regrets, in a way that honors the weird spirit of the show and does not surrender to making trite requests for our sympathy. It's been 90 years since *The Jazz Singer* gave us sound on the silver screen, and although it's hard to imagine film without that cinematic element, it's fun to be taken back to a time when it was not there and reimagine how a new story can be told through these lenses of the past.

Jaws

*"Sometimes that shark he looks right into ya. Right into your eyes.
And, you know, the thing about a shark... he's got lifeless eyes.
Black eyes. Like a doll's eyes. When he comes at ya, doesn't seem to
be living...."*
- Peter Benchley and Carl Gottlieb (script)

How many films radically recalibrate what you think you know
about the world? I still feel <u>Jaws</u>' impact almost 40 years after its
release forever changed the consciousness of would-be beach
dwellers, a feeling I share with my brother whose comment on how
the film is probably the scariest of all time because of how it gives
you real-world fears is dead on. This is not due to the body count
(three deaths are spaced almost equilaterally throughout the film at
its beginning, middle, and end). Nor is it due to the spectacle of a
giant shark with an affinity for boats and a heat-seeking focus on
eating and surviving. And as classic as the team of Richard
Dreyfuss, Roy Scheider, and Robert Shaw is, it is not the
performances (but, okay, few things are cooler than that shot where
Steven Spielberg does a sort of foreground and background spatial
collapse zoom-in to Scheider's eyes, which say more than words
ever could).

No, for me it is the lingering dread that runs throughout the film. The
sense that you know some chaotic monster is lurking beneath the
murky blue waters, out of sight, and almost guaranteed to appear
when you least expect it. It doesn't matter how many times I watch
this film, I still jump at different parts and think about it when I go to
the beach. At the end of the shark-chum day, it shows Spielberg as a
student of the Hitchcockian anticipation is worse than the bang
school, as well as an auteur in the mode of the 1970s filmmakers
able to tell dark stories through their own unique visions, a prelude
of blood and saltwater-churned chaos to a storied career.

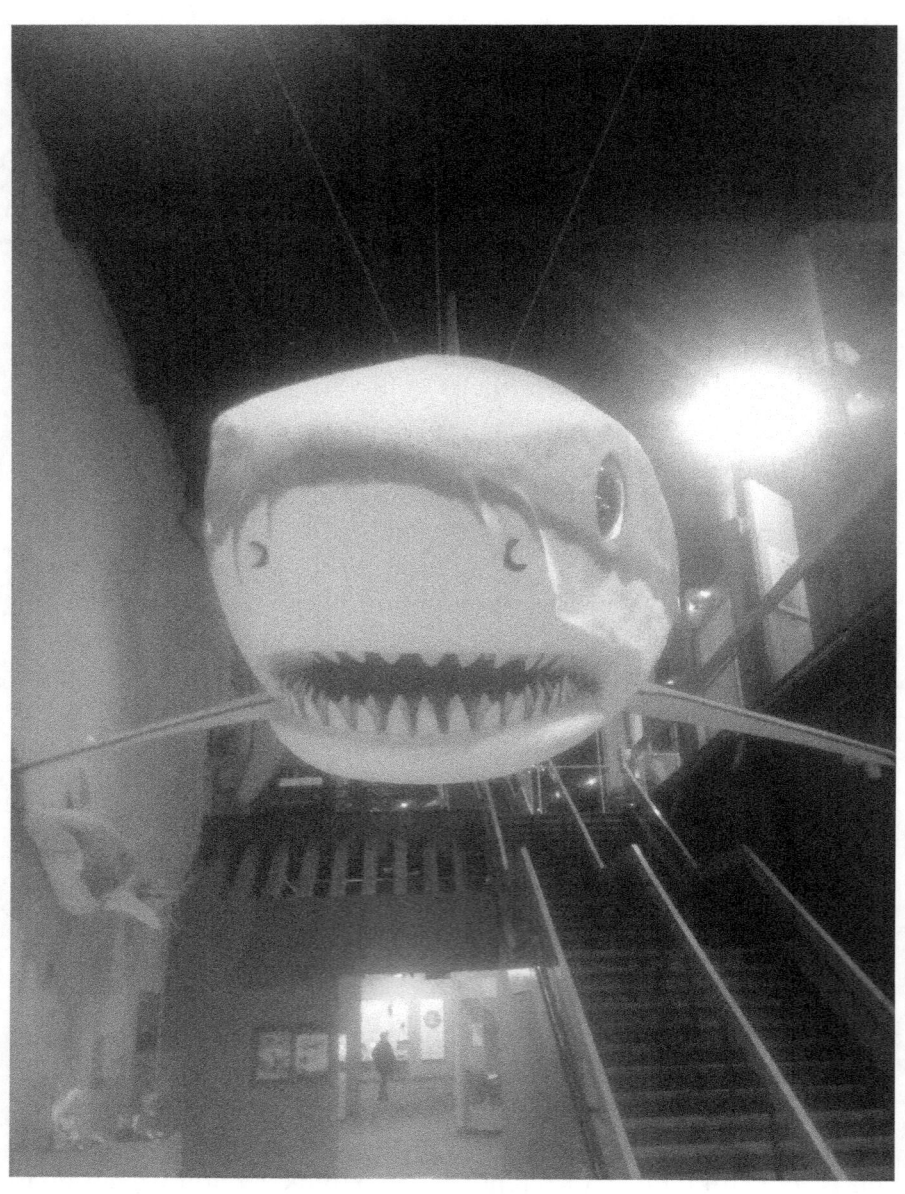

The South Carolina State Museum, Columbia

Act II: The Plot Thickens (Like a Milkshake That Should Just Be Called Ice Cream (No You Can't Drink it, Daniel Day-Lewis))

Int. Diner- Day

The Top 15 Animal Performances of All Time

1. Free Willy. Can't downplay the difficulty of the climactic jump.
2. Clyde from Every Which Way But Loose. Clint Eastwood's truck-driving co-pilot orangutan is also a wingman for the ages.
3. Sully "Steven" Seagull from The Shallows. Director Jaume Collet-Sera[15] chose to eschew CGI and animatronics and use a real seagull for the performance. "I didn't know it at the time that I was working with him," noted Collet-Sera, "but he was kind of like the Marlon Brando of seagulls."
4. Babe(s). Played by a cast of pigs, the Babe character goes from bright-eyed idealist to crying cynic to triumphant sheep pig, with each performance in perfect synchronicity with another.
5. Old Yeller, who is maybe the John Wayne of film dogs.
6. Toto from The Wizard of Oz, the Charlie Chaplin of dogs.
7. Baxter from Anchorman. Lemme tell you, Adam McKay didn't find it amazing when he pooped all over the first print of film reels.
8. Einstein from Back to the Future. Did you know Einstein is technically the first time traveler ever?
9. Buddy from Air Bud. I still don't understand how he can shoot a basketball with his head.
10. Winter from Dolphin Tale. Actually played by a real dolphin with a Twitter account.
11. Jaws. Although an animatronic version was used for most of the film, actual footage of a shark was used for the cage scene.
12. Hooch in Turner and Hooch. Hooch was actually set to win Best Supporting Dog, but Tom Hanks sabotaged his Oscar campaign in a fit of uncharacteristic jealousy.
13. The Tiger in The Hangover was said to have become friends with Mike Tyson on set.
14. The Birds. Every. Last. One. Of. Them.
15. The MGM Lion. Said to be slightly jealous of the Wilhelm scream.

---

[15] *Vulture*: "The Breakout Movie Star of the Summer is the Seagull from The Shallows", interview by Kyle Buchanan.

Exploring the End of Sausage Party- What Does it All Mean, Man?

If you go and see *Sausage Party*, the 2016 Seth Rogen/Evan Goldberg animated romp featuring the dark trials and tribulations of anthropomorphized food in a grocery market (with a little dash of *The Brave Little Toaster*, *Toy Story 3*, and some super dark anime film I haven't seen but know is out there), the price of admission is worth it alone to see the food orgy. If you've seen it, you know what I mean. If you haven't, well, whatthehellareyoudoinggoseeitrightnowitsoneofthegreatestscenesinth ehistoryofcinematheLumièrebrotherswouldbeproudorhorrifiedprobab lyhorrifiedbutMélièswouldbeproud.

Okay, now that's out of my system, I want to get to the ending, which I think is more up for debate. Over the course of the film (or maybe from the beginning if you are already inclined to view *Sausage Party* in a certain light), it becomes clearer that this story may be an allegorical depiction of our own struggles with finding meaning in the world, and how religion (referred to as the Great Beyond in the film) is used to ease those struggles at the cost of a greater truth- life is painful and we all die. A group of imperishable foods, such as the Firewater Chief (voiced by Bill Hader (he is also the shady bottle of tequilla), a twinkie bar, and a Pop Tart type food, promoted this message to protect their own way of life, as a way of being outside the normal cycle of death and destruction, much as the hegemonic structure of money and power has flowed through the particular channels of a system set up long ago. The perishables- the franks, buns, tacos, bagels, mustards and others- are bound to the cycle of doom, and one figures at the end, even though they have won the food fight, staved off the true horrors of the Great Beyond, and experienced a true Bacchanalian festival of delight, that they are still bound to the grim realities of their world- they will be eaten, rot away, or disintegrate. This is undeniably a sad ending, but it would have still a ring of truth to it and would have worked with much of what went before (e.g. a guy gets his head chopped off and that's not the most terrifying moment of the film). That the filmmakers end up softening the blow with a, this-is-just-an-alternate-reality-message, felt like a missed opportunity for me, as it let us walk away from the theater not really wondering or worrying about the fate of the foods. It's not that we don't know this already from our own lives, we just don't have the luxury of zapping into an alternate dimension yet.

This isn't all to say I was ultimately disappointed with the film. That there is this much to discuss in a movie about talking hot dogs (and really, to be quite frank, there's a lot more I haven't gotten to) is pretty amazing. There are moments of horror, comedy, and introspection, all gut-wrenching alike, and it is an experience you will likely remember for some time to come, at least until after your next grocery store trip, or bath salts experience.

Downpressor Man: Django Unchained, the NRA, and the Hollywood Blame Game

"I mean we have blood-soaked films out there, like American Psycho, Natural Born Killers. They're aired like propaganda loops on Splatterdays and every single day... And then they all have the nerve to call it entertainment. But is that what it really is? Isn't fantasizing about killing people as a way to get your kicks really the filthiest form of pornography?"
–Wayne LaPierre, Executive Vice President of the National Rifle Association

If you are so inclined, you can go to the NRA National Firearms Museum in Fairfax, Virginia and head to the William P. Ruger Gallery. Nowadays there you will find a rotating exhibit called Hollywood Guns[16]. The exhibit has seven cases of guns from films through the ages of our cinema. You've probably seen some of them on Splatterday. Maybe they get you off.

Quentin Tarantino's latest, Django Unchained, is one of the more violent films you will ever see released in the mainstream. There's whipping, ravenous dogs, a hammer-to-the-head execution, explosions, and shooting. Lots and lots of shooting.

Does Tarantino glorify violence here? Sure. But he is well within his bounds as an artist to express himself however he pleases. He does not condone murder, nor should these films be viewed as a call-to-arms for our society to kill more people. We as a society should be able to separate what happens on screen with the choices we make to lead positive lives. If you think this stuff is bad, don't watch it. Moderation is another possibility.

---

[16] I wrote this in the winter of 2013, but as of summer 2017 (!) they still have this exhibit there.

45

The second we start dictating what people can or cannot do in their art, or what people can or cannot be entertained by, is the second we completely miss the point and make the problem worse. Art should be free, and show us the best and worst of what's out there, not what some numbskull has the nerve to say to anyone in the wake of one of the most horrific tragedies of the modern age (how about some respect for, I don't know, the families and the community of a town that will never be the same?). Audiences should be free to take in what they choose to watch. Last time I checked, freedom of speech came before the right to bear arms in the Bill of Rights[17].

---

[17] *The following were used as sources/inspiration for this piece:
1. John Aravosis, "NRA Web site glorifies violent Hollywood movies after NRA chief criticizes violent Hollywood movies," *Americablog,*
http://americablog.com/2013/01/nra-glorifies-violent-hollywood-movies-after-criticizing-violent-hollywood-movies.html
2. Tom Diaz, "Bloody Reel- How the NRA and the Gun Industry Exploit Violent Movies to Sell Guns…and More Guns," *Fairly Civil,* January 2, 2013,
http://tomdiazgunsandgangs.com/2013/01/02/bloody-reel-how-the-nra-and-the-gun-industry-exploit-violent-movies-to-sell-guns-and-more-guns/
3. Tom Morello, "Paul Ryan is the Embodiment of the Machine Our Music Rages Against," *Rolling Stone,* August 16, 2012,
http://www.rollingstone.com/music/news/tom-morello-paul-ryan-is-the-embodiment-of-the-machine-our-music-rages-against-20120816

Fear and Loathing in Puerto Rico (<u>The Rum Diary</u>)

"There's a thin veneer between the dream and the reality.[18]"

I. A Brief Modern History of the Island

Puerto Rico is an island in the Caribbean that is now a U.S. territory. That status has been a critical political issue since the U.S. took over the island from the Spanish at the turn of the nineteenth century (said U.S. invasion was sparked by a false claim from the yellow press about why the U.S. battleship *Maine* sunk). People there have been split over whether to become an official U.S. state, remain a territory, or become a sovereign nation. Being a territory for now means the island exists somewhere between being a part of the U.S. and on its own in the world.

This limbo status makes sense in a way that speaks to some truths about our democracy. It is a classic American political compromise, a working solution that caters to both sides, and even creates a new one that is fine with the status quo, but does not actually provide a definitive solution. In some ways this is fine, perhaps even beneficial to the island, as it gets to continue to benefit from being a part of the U.S., yet retains important cultural elements that makes it a unique and unforgettable place. In other words, the debate's the thing. As long as there are people arguing about what Puerto Rico should be in the world, there is the opportunity for meaningful action and the positive change that democratic societies should enact[19].

---

[18] Hunter S. Thompson, *The Rum Diary*.

[19] It should be noted that this situation gets increasingly more complicated with each passing day, with situations like the Puerto Rican government-debt crisis and the recent Zika virus driving a wrench in the argument that the territorial status of the island is in any way beneficial (from what I understand this designation means the island gets less aid from the U.S. government and less funds to combat the virus, which is doubly problematic because the island was set up as a place where U.S. businesses could gain tax breaks if they were to have residence on these grounds, which sounds like it could possibly bring some money into the local

47

II. A Brief History of My Experience in Puerto Rico

Dancing and drinking down cobblestone streets in the night. Flying on ziplines over rainforests and thinking about dying. Riding back from white sand beaches as the sun falls. Feeling an acute level of despair on those beaches, that despite all the beauty around you, it doesn't really matter... Killing time in the beach bar before the boat takes you back to the mainland. Touring rum empires inspired by hanging bats. Walking with lizards among old castle ramparts...Vestiges of New Orleans in old San Juan, beach communities in Los Angeles, but this felt like a totally different place than the rest of America.

III. A Briefer History of My Experience in Puerto Rico

Upon leaving she wished me luck with the ukelele. I haven't played the ukelele much since.

III. The Rum Diary Film

The Rum Diary film was by and large a flop, but it remains to me an interesting type of flop, both for and not for the reasons above. Adapted from the Hunter S. Thompson book, *The Rum Diary* tells the story of reporter Paul Kemp (a fictionalized version of Hunter S. Thompson played by Johnny Depp) who leaves America to join a newspaper in Puerto Rico, seeking refuge from the banalities and ugliness of Nixon's America. An entrepreneur named Sanderson (a role in Aaron Eckhart's wheelhouse) wants Kemp to pump out propaganda that would help fuel the development of a resort on one of Puerto Rico's islands[20]. Kemp wants to write journalism and not

---

economy unless these same businesses distribute their products and services off the island, without funneling an equitable share of the profits back into the place that lets them thrive in the first place). I'm summarizing this from a *Rolling Stone* article from summer 2016 that goes into way more depth and is better than my abstracted analysis: "Zika, the Epidemic at America's Door," by Janet Reitman.
[20] I could not tell which one, as the developers were deliberately coy to retain secrecy. A quick shot of the resort made it seem like it was housed on the island of Culebra due to the snake-like curve on an edge of the land. However, Culebra in

be directed to write in a particular slant that would undermine the most critical aspect of his work: the truth. In the end though, he finds that going against the grain of these peoples' desires is the very truth that needs to come across in his work.

It is a tricky job to depict the life of a writer on screen, yet in showing us Thompson's world in his formative years in *The Rum Diary*, director Bruce Robinson gives the audience insight into the major influences of a particularly idiosyncratic writer's tone, a pioneer of the Gonzo-strain of New Journalism. He provides us a Thompson origin story of sorts that is entertaining in the Gonzo style for which the Good Doctor became famous (the scene when he breathes fire while being chased by the locals from the restaurant is pure, 128 proof Thompson), yet doesn't shy away from showing us the hard truths inextricable to this condition.

Thompson's doppelganger sees that what he has left behind from the mainland is still with him on the island. Kemp is amongst people who have left the U.S. but still have an aggressive, economically-driven mindset and view the island more as an opportunity for Manifest destiny-esque expansion and less as a place inhabited by a unique people and their beautiful culture. Kemp's decision to go against this mindset reflects his own passionately held beliefs. From the ashes of his own troubles with drug abuse, he fights the fire of greed and self-serving institutions through an instrument that often is more powerful than the sword. It has long been a challenge to depict a writer on screen, but Robinson makes a strong effort of capturing a chaotic voice by depicting Kemp's struggles on an "ocean of money" in a way that gives us an understanding of his inner turmoil and what will drive this person in the future.

Reading Thompson is like going into the mind of a madman. You will not come out the same on the other end because he is, as Kemp

actuality benefits from special zoning laws that limit the scale and type of development that would be necessary for a resort to be built. Since these were put in place by the U.S. military before the time of the story, this may rule out Culebra, although it would not surprise me that some people out there would have wanted to get around that loophole at some point in time.

promises toward the end of the film, a "voice filled with ink and rage," who is as unmerciful in his attacks on the bastards of the world as he is with his body and the circumstances he gleefully throws himself into. That can be a hard thing to reconcile- that we are supposed to be on the side of someone who comes off as unsympathetic in his own right - but in figuring out how we feel about those actions, empathizing with the motives at least, if not always the means by which they come into the fray, we can take something away from the experience. By giving us this framework in a cinematic forum, Robinson has made a valuable contribution to his art.

But, you ask, if you appreciate the film because you went there, the film alludes to but does not explain a history, and the protagonist requires some additional unraveling behind the scenes, then does the film really stand on its own right? Yes, dear reader and viewer, faithful citizen of a free nation, you may be right, but you may do well to remember the words of the wise man-[21]

---

[21] *Editor's note*- Upon receiving this article, the fax machine sputtered out and cut off the final sentence. Attempts to reach the writer have been unsuccessful.

Marathon: The Patriots Day Bombing

Not on the way into many movies will you pause just past the usher and wait for a man with a prosthetic leg to sort things out and meet up with his film going companion, who happens to be on crutches. Nor are there many times when you are at a screening trying to figure out who the director of the film is, only to speculate on a person who happens to have a main role in the film and is someone who ran a marathon after losing his leg in a bombing at the same event only a few years earlier. There probably aren't many times when you will see a cute service dog and realize the depth of that service dog's bad-assery extends to helping a couple find some semblance of joy in a world irrevocably altered by the hateful actions of those who would want to set off bombs near children.

All this is to say it was beyond humbling to attend a recent screening of *Marathon: The Patriots Day Bombing*, a new documentary about the Boston Marathon bombings that was released in late 2016. Directed by Ricki Stern and Annie Sundberg, *Marathon: The Patriots Day Bombing* tells the story of the 2013 Boston Marathon bombing, notably its consequences in both the public arena and the private lives of those forever changed from what happened on that fateful April morning. It is perhaps the latter here that made this documentary unique for me, since it makes the film more than just a re-telling of a story that will probably seem familiar for most viewers, albeit one told here with some compelling and chilling footage of the bombings themselves and the Tsarneav brothers, lingering with people near the finish line, approaching a police car around the corner of an MIT building, emerging from a boat, bloodied and beaten.

Stern and Sundberg splice coverage of the Boston Marathon investigation with depictions of several survivors, focusing on married couple Jessica Kensky and Patrick Downes, mother and daughter Celeste and Sydney Corcoran, and JP Norden. Over the course of the film we see how these people recover, see how they learn to walk, run, work, and live again, handling not only the considerable physical pain of their circumstances, but the mental anguish of knowing their lives will never be the same. We also get insight into the lives of others who were impacted by the tragedy, from the photographer of a front-page shot seen round the world, whose guilt over his actions that day led him to document the recovery of the Corcorans, to the Richard family, whose son, Martin, was one of the four fatalities, and who all suffered in their own way, yet wanted to see Dzhokhar Tsarneav spend a life in prison instead of the death penalty, knowing his death would not heal their wounds, and that the prolonged machinations required for execution would draw out their pain.

During the Q and A after the film, I was struck by something that Downes said in response to a question touching on the other tragedies that have seemingly occurred with increasing frequency in recent times. He noted how it is common for us to show a lot of empathy in the immediate aftermath of such events, but how after a week or so we start to forget about the victims and they fade into the background. It is important to remember them long after, he said, and I think films such as *Marathon: The Patriots Day Bombing* do an admirable job in following through on that conviction.

Bambi's Echoes

Bambi is notorious for having one of the saddest moments ever captured on film- when the titular fawn loses his mother and is led into the snowy darkness by the Great Prince of the Forest. While this is true, I think there is more to <u>Bambi</u> than meets the eye. There is a genre-defying thread that runs throughout the film. Sure, it's an animated kids movie. But as far as conventions go, it is anything but ordinary. We witness the birth and growth of a deer who continues the cycle of life. The ending is the same as the beginning. Things change but only because they have to, because it is the natural progression. Nothing really happens except life. You are separated from your parents, you have to find your way in the world, and soon you have to be the protector for the next generation. It's funny when the owl walks in the air and twirls, mimicking spring love. It's strangely subversive when you find out Flower's a dude. It's telling when you realize the enemy is Man, is us, the ones watching the film who will probably not take anything away from the experience except that a cute deer lost his mom. We kill the animals, we burn the forest, and all you see of us is our tents, all you hear is our gunshots. It's mysterious when the camera leads you through the forest and you see the animals gathering because a new prince is born. It's hopeful when Bambi leaps to safety. It is a symphony of lightning flashes, mole tunnels, and antlers crashing. And it is sad when Bambi calls out for his mom and she is not there and the snow falls as he cries as the Great Prince tells him she is not there anymore. It is so fucking sad.

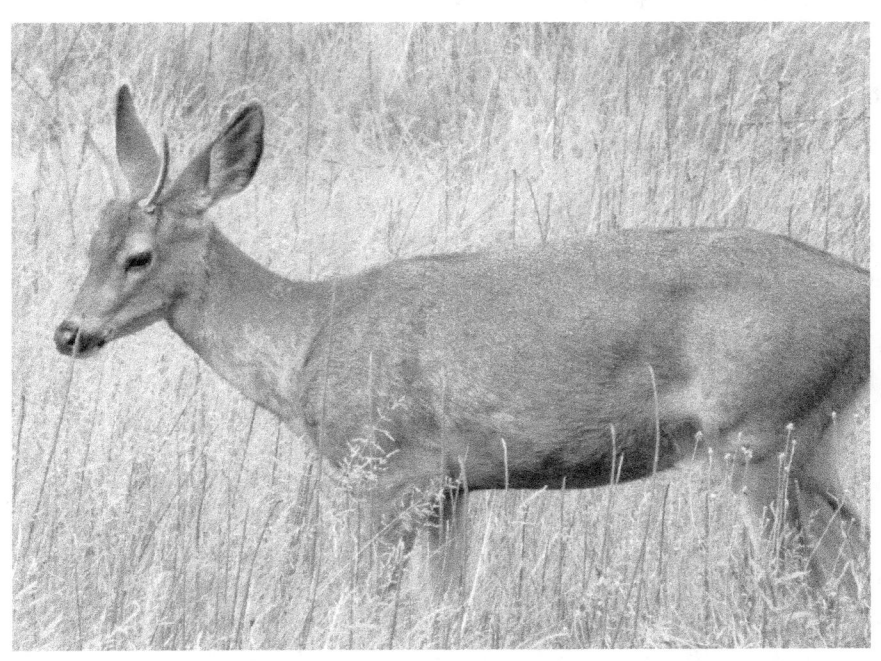

Yosemite National Park

Grumpiest Old Men List

Seeing Stephen Lang scare the holy hell out of would-be home-robbers in <u>Don't Breathe</u> got me thinking- who are the most cantankerous old men to have graced the silver screen? It's a surprisingly rich list, even though I had to kick out Oscar the Grouch[22] since he's primarily a TV character and I'm not worried about him getting access to a computer to troll me:

1. <u>Grumpy Old Men</u>'s Walter Matthau and Jack Lemmon. They were so grouchy they even made a <u>Grumpier Old Men</u>, lending even more credence to the idea that there's never been a sequel idea that Hollywood execs didn't like.
2. Lionel Barrymore in <u>It's a Wonderful Life</u>- the miserliest of miserly old men seems even crankier in old black and white film.
3. Harrison Ford in <u>Air Force One</u>: "Get off my plane!"
4. Clint Eastwood in <u>Gran Torino</u>: "Get off my porch!"
5. Burgess Meredith in <u>Rocky</u>. Meredith also plays the Penguin in the 1960s Batman television series (RIP Mayor West).
6. Carl Frederickson in <u>Up</u>, whose crusty surface belies a heart of pixelated gold.
7. Danny Glover in <u>Lethal Weapon</u>: Claims he's too old for this shit, even as he kicks ass in doing said shit.
8. Robert De Nero in <u>Meet the Parents</u>: "I have nipples Greg…" remains one of the great rhetorical counter-blows in film history.
9. Al Pacino as Lieutenant Colonel Frank Slade in <u>Scent of a Woman</u>: Even knows the scent of the readers still here.
10. Stephen Lang in <u>Don't Breathe</u>: Not as much grumpy as he is bat-shit crazy.

---

[22] Now at 47 years old, the Grouch is well into the age threshold necessitated for this list (he might have been older at the start of the series). Still, he's a TV character and this is a movie list (I'm looking at you too, the Grinch!). Get outta here Oscar!

The Biggest Snub Ever? Idris Elba in <u>Beasts of No Nation</u>

The first thing you notice is the shoulders, hanging low and loose, blades bobbing up and down as the body that holds them saunters from side to side. He moves across the ground in a carefully controlled dance, holding the full attention of the crowd on screen and the audience off of it, and when he speaks it is with a smooth cadence in step with his movements, inviting, charismatic, menacing, maybe even insane. It is with this mix of characteristics that Idris Elba gives a riveting, unforgettable performance in *Beasts of No Nation*, showing one of our best actors out there at the top of his game. Too bad it wasn't even nominated for an Oscar in 2015.

Elba's case as the best snub ever is heightened by the fact that he is now the first person to win the Screen Actor's Guild award and not even be nominated for the same performance. Now does any of this matter when you watch the movie? Of course not. Elba's performance is still amazing and is not diminished by his exclusion from Academy Award consideration.

At the end of the day the Oscars is just another awards show, more prestigious then the others perhaps, but still just a ceremony to hand out gold statues to people. Personally, I like to view it as a fun celebration of film, and even though that may be an odd way to characterize 2016's edition, which may be more aptly remembered as having spawned the Twitter topic #OscarsSoWhite, that's really all it is, warts and all.

The Young Person's Guide to the Cinematic Romance (<u>Moonrise Kingdom</u>)

"I love you but you don't know what you're talking about."
-Wes Anderson and Roman Coppola (script)

The opening song to <u>Moonrise Kingdom</u> is "The Young Person's Guide to the Orchestra" by Benjamin Britten. In the classical piece a child teaches the listener about the different instruments that will appear in the song. As the film opens, the song plays as the viewer sees the different rooms in the homes of Suzy (Kara Heyward) and Sam (Jared Gilman). When the next song comes on, the setting shifts to a campground on New Penzance Island and the story unfolds.

As much as <u>Moonrise Kingdom</u> is about the young romance between Suzy and Sam, the film is a canvas for Wes Anderson to paint on with his cast of colorful characters. There are Anderson troupe regulars Bill Murray and Jason Schwartzman and newcomers like Edward Norton[23], who strays from the motions of the more serious men he tends to portray and instead gives a funny and touching performance as Scout Master Ward. It is a testament to Murray as an actor that he is able to fall into his role here as Suzy's father and still produce the laughs we all expect from him in a more subtle manner, as when he discovers his daughter in an embarrassing situation.

---

[23] Who thankfully returned in Anderson's hit, *The Grand Budapest Hotel*. Here's what I wrote about that one: *Inspired by the writings of Stefan Zweig, Wes Anderson's latest is a funny, rollicking epic that highlights the director's talents particularly well, from the set design featuring such items as cotton-candy pink wallpaper and the prized Boy with Apple painting, to the zipping camera style that mimics the movements of the characters and the plot's progression, taking you down an Olympic slalom and past snow-capped fields and icy rivers, now marked by the shadow of the Nazi presence. Put together,* <u>The Grand Budapest Hotel</u> *shows you how a part of the world went from one era into another and lost something intrinsically important to the human spirit along the way.*

Bruce Willis plays Murray's rival and fits in seamlessly into the Anderson ensemble through his own dry humor and optimistic pessimist identity (the cousin of the underrated overrated player). Willis may just be a new Anderson regular unless Sylvester Stallone keeps making Expendables movies[24]. And he may well be accompanied as a regular by newcomer Gilman, who comes off here as a charming cross of Schwartzman and Peter Billingsley as Ralphie in A Christmas Story.

As the child tells us at the end of "The Young Person's Guide to the Orchestra" the instruments converge to form a full symphony of sound. If the performances of the men in Moonrise Kingdom are the "call" of a classic jazz call and response pattern, the women are undoubtedly the response. Kara Heyward is mesmerizing as Suzy and I could not help feel somewhat creepy for being attracted to her. She is impressive both for displaying an instinctive grace and a thoughtful attentiveness to the challenges of the role and the actors around her. I was surprised at how far Anderson goes with the character through her dress, poses, stares, and a memorable waltz on the beach; he takes the bold strokes of his art to the edges of social acceptability. It is no wonder that Sam is attracted to Suzy like the northern pole of a magnet is to its southern end. Heyward also shines in her scenes with her mother Laura, who is played by Frances McDormand. When Laura gives Suzy a bath midway through the

[24] This is one of the strangely more prophetic passages I've ever written, albeit for reasons I never could have predicted. Moonrise Kingdom and The Expendables 2 were released in 2012. In 2013, Willis backed out of being in The Expendables 3 over an apparent salary dispute, prompting Stallone to tweet: "GREEDY AND LAZY . . . A SURE FORMULA FOR CAREER FAILURE." In 2014, *The Grand Budapest Hotel* came out, sans Willis, but, more importantly, he appeared to have acquiesced with Stallone, who wrote in November of that year, "Made up with BRUCE W. A stand up guy, my mistake...." As of the time of this writing, in late 2016, there are rumors and hopes for a 4th Expendables movie, with Arnold Schawarznegger saying, "I told Sly to write another one or have someone else write another one," (in other words, "jass dooo it! Gimme the moooovie!"), and while it is unclear whether Willis will appear in it, there are rumors of an appearance from the Biebs, much to the chagrin of Jason Statham and Selena Gomez. There is no word on Willis appearing in another Anderson movie, much to my chagrin.

film, she sees her daughter look down at a book that was meant to be hidden. Do the two come to a begrudging understanding? Or do they both begrudgingly accept that which cannot be fully understood? Although the lines and iconic displays of theatrical movements from our favorite actors are often what stand out in a film, there are those subtle expressions and silent exchanges that may resonate in our viewing subconscious on an even deeper level. When the child tells us the instruments are about to come together we see the two lovers in the same room. They play and come apart, and we are left with a painting of the place where they danced and embraced, a memento of the most beautiful art.

Short Films in 2013

If you are growing increasingly cynical about the quality of the mainstream and prominent independent feature-length films, not to mention those nominated for Oscars, then may I recommend you dabble in the short film? Similar to how short stories must be economic in how they use their limited duration, short films are able to convey a lot in the time they are given, are great forums for creative concepts and experimental storytelling, and are able to show the essence of a slice of life. Over the years, I have taken to watching the Oscar nominated short films[25] at the E. St. Landmark Theater in Washington, D.C[26]. In 2013, I was particularly struck by the quality of the short live-action films. The following is taken from my Oscar preview of that year:

All of the films in 2013 would have been worthwhile winners. Death of a Shadow is a surreal Belgium film that reminded me of one of the best short film adaptations I have ever seen, Occurrence at Owl Creek Bridge, which was made back in the day as a Twilight Zone special[27]. Buzkashi Boys introduced me to the Afghan sport of Buzkashi through the stirring images of horseback riders galloping through the snow and a young child who dreams of becoming a rider to rise out of poverty. Asad is sort of an ironic take of the Old Man and the Sea, in which a Somali child goes out to sea and reels in a magical sea creature. The filmmakers deserve a ton of credit for the lightning-quick pacing as well as what is perhaps the film's major achievement of subverting our assumptions about the place and culture that is generally associated with spawning many of the notorious pirates of Western Africa.

---

[25] D.C. also has a Shorts Film Festival every year, which is something I suspect exists in other metropolitan areas.

[26] These films are also more readily available on streaming platforms, so definitely keep an eye out for them throughout the year and particularly around awards-season time.

[27] And was itself an adaptation of Ambrose Bierce's classic short story.

For all the talk about the big awards in 2013, I think the Live Action Short category may have been the closest race. My hunch is that the voters will go with Henry because of its similarity to the trending Amour, its relevance to the aging the voters are going through, and for how the classical music creates a serious, dignified mood for the film that gives it an aura of more serious art. I liked this more than Amour because it took the risk of going into the subject's mind, and provided a sentimentality and warmth missing from Amour, which I thought exploited a depressing subject to the detriment of the viewer. I hope the voters choose Curfew, although I cannot deny my subjective inclinations make me lean toward picking this film in what I think is a better race than the one for Best Picture because of the range, experimentation, quality, and pound-for-pound value of screen time of these films. You write what you know and relate to what makes you feel, and nothing evoked quite the range of emotions I had watching Curfew, whether they be joy, laughter, or tears. The scene when the little girl shimmy dances down the bowling lane is one of my favorites from recent years, and I expect the lead actors, Shawn Christensen and Fatima Ptacek, to go on to do great things. I highly recommend you go on iTunes and buy the film for $2 (I will even reimburse you if you do not like it). Seriously, stop reading this book and go see it[28].

---

[28] This means you, Steve!

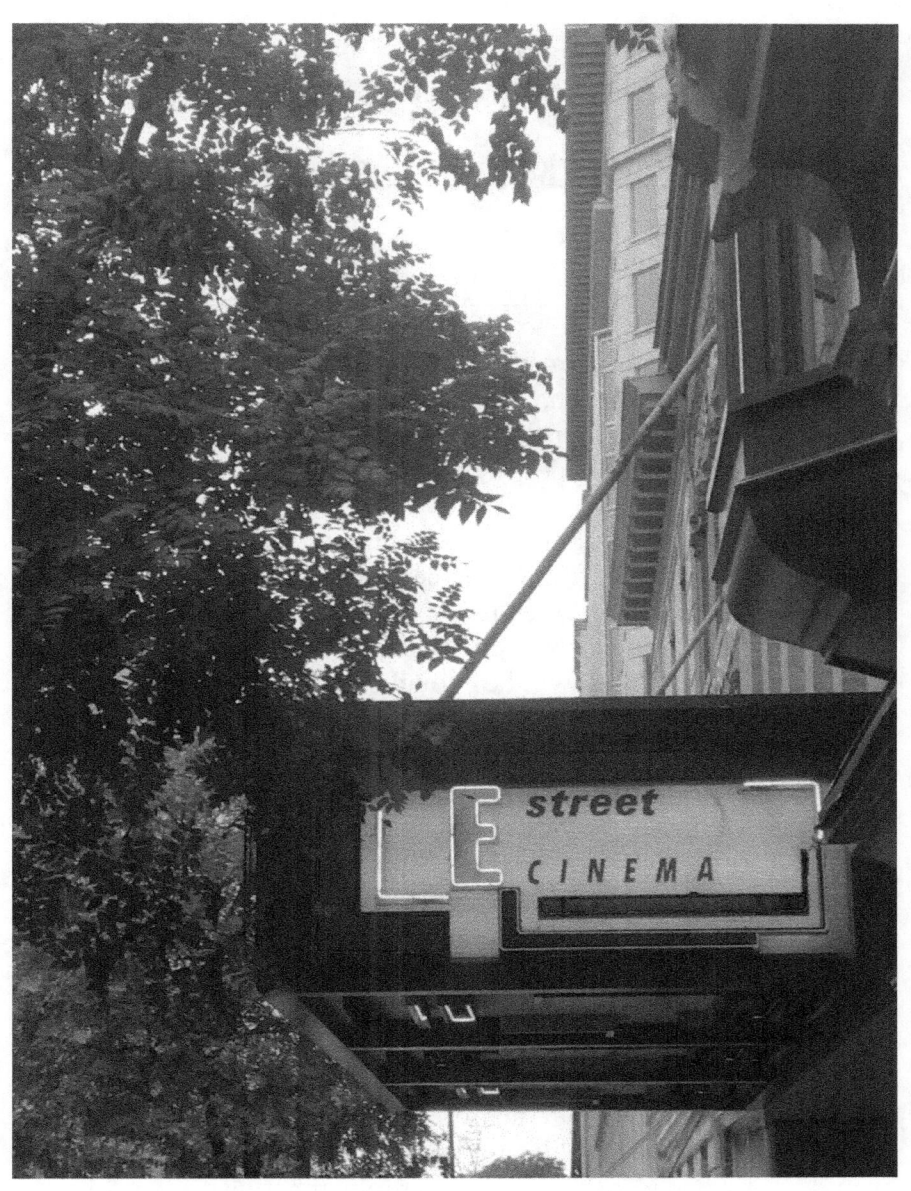

Weighing **<u>The Perks of Being a Wallflower</u>** Adaptation

I read Steven Chbosky's[29] <u>The Perks of Being a Wallflower</u> on a road trip after it was given to me by a friend. I devoured the book in a day as my family and I made our way from Baltimore to Annapolis to the Chesapeake Bay (ahh the lingering days of yesteryear, when one could more readily tune out the white noise from the burgeoning technical mediums set to destroy us).

For those who have read the book heading into its adaptation, it is hard to detach yourself from the experience of having read the book as you watch the movie. Even if you read the book a long time ago, chances are it still lingers somewhere in your brain; perhaps only the idea of reading the book will be enough to control your perception of what the movie should be or how it can be successful in its cinematic form. A lot of this, I surmise, has to do with nostalgia; books, like other forms of art, bring back certain memories of being in a time and place. I fell pray to this nostalgia when watching <u>The Perks of Being a Wallflower</u> adaptation, expecting the film to give me the same feeling the book did. How could it though? If the book brought about powerful feelings because of what I was going through and where I was going, and those feelings inevitably changed, then how could I expect to feel the same way about a movie working from the same source? In an odd way, I realize the movie may have done exactly what it was supposed to do for me now, which is bringing me back to those days, to remember reading on the road, thinking of someone who existed within and without me, wondering where it all would go. I wonder if I will remember remembering all this 8 years from now. Maybe it will be on TV.

The old the book-was-better-than-the-movie trope ran through my

---

[29] Chbosky also directed the film here, which makes me wonder whether all adaptations, no matter how well-intentioned, are all kinda doomed.

head throughout <u>The Perks of Being a Wallflower</u>. Afterwards, I found myself vacillating between liking the film for the subjective reasons I have just described, and not liking it for more objective reasons.

My essential problem with this film stems from the depiction of the protagonist[30]. As the narrator who is writing you the letters in the story, Charlie is the entryway into this world, he is the wallflower of the title, who listens to everyone yet does not reveal much of his own hang-ups. On one hand this is realistic because people are, for the most part, as Charles Dickens[31] once said "mysteries," and you have to get to know them to peel away some of the subterfuge. On the other hand, these mysteries do not end with the simple unmasking of the criminal; they can be muddled, lead to dead ends, or make you discover more about yourself. In <u>The Perks of Being a Wallflower</u>, Charlie carries the trauma of his aunt's death even though he was not responsible for it. At least, this is what I think is the case. The film shows flashbacks to the death after a few emotional scenes; Charlie mentions it when he's high, and Charlie and his brother talk about it on his birthday. There is certainly nothing wrong with feeling sad about the loss of a loved one. I just think the use of the death as a device to make Charlie a tortured adolescent trivializes the tribulations you go through at that age; why does there need to be a

---

[30]Another problem I have is with the Secret Santa reveal scene. How on earth could these people afford all that stuff? Patrick gets Charlie a whole new outfit, including a suit. Charlie gets Patrick a smorgasbord of presents, and still has change left over to give everyone else cool gifts, including $40 of the $50 his dad gave him for some gift certificate to Mary-Elizabeth. Sam gets Charlie a ballin' typewriter (another issue I had: how could he help her study for the SATs when he was still a freshman? Was he that gifted and did she not learn ANYTHING in high school? I found this completely unbelievable; also why is the loner always brilliant, and how did the nerdy freshman dude get the hot senior? Emma Watson would have been completely untouchable at my high school). Years after seeing it this still makes no sense to me. These people were shilling out fancy gifts like there was no tomorrow. Back in the day, I could barely afford the value menu at Wendy's.

[31] Dickens was also the answer to Paul Rudd's question about who made the first trade paperbacks. Why hasn't Paul Rudd played an inspirational teacher before? We need more roles for Paul Rudd besides friggin Ant-Man and the token middle-aged man in a Judd Apatow comedy.

reason for angst? There are a whole variety of causes that can make you feel depressed; how making out with Emma Watson could trigger a suicide attempt is beyond me. Maybe this all was in the story, maybe I am completely misinterpreting everything, but my impression was that Charlie did not need to be explained. And high school is a strange enough place to literally parse out all those harboring demons.

Maybe this all still leads back to a subjective assessment. I like the film because I remember how the book helped me once upon a time and maybe the movie can help me now. I do not like the film because I cannot fully relate to Charlie's experiences even in those memories. I like the film because I want to remember my past that way. I do not like the film because I know my past was different. I am happy there is art like this to escape into. I am sad because I want this to be real. Who knows? You accept the film you think you deserve.

Captain Fantastic

A commenter on an article I once posted for *TheOneRing.net* said the piece was nothing more than a paean, and lacked any sort of critical, balanced perspective on the matter. She was completely right. I'm an unabashed lover of movies and have a hard time bringing myself to completely hating anything I see (see my recent *Batman vs. Superman* piece). This also manifested in a recent workplace conversation in which one of my coworkers lambasted the last *Hobbit* film as one of the worst he had ever seen, to which I could only reply, "I dunno, I kinda liked it."

One major contributing factor to this is that as an amateur film critic I have to pick and choose what I see and it's really not that different then the film enthusiast who goes to see what he wants any given week. Professional critics see a ton of movies and there's undoubtedly a lot of crap out there that gets made. It's a life I imagine must be similar to the one a bartender at a music venue I once met had- you see shows every night and eventually they kind of blur together- takes a lot to stand out and the good ones eventually rise to the top but it's not without good measure.

Anyhue, this is all to say I fucking loved *Captain Fantastic*, the madcap, irreverent black comedy from writer-director Matt Ross (also an actor with roles including, amazingly enough, a great performance as Gavin Belson on Silicon Valley). I have a hard time bestowing anything but superlatives on it and would proclaim it a lock for Best Picture if that didn't seem antithetical to the film's anti-authoritarian, free-thinking, unschooling, cosmically unspooling, Noam Chomsky celebrating, consumerist drone denouncing whirligig tour de force vibe.

Viggo Mortensen is electric in the lead role, ironies about a movie star denouncing the corporate ills of our world notwithstanding. As

Ben, the patriarch of a family living on the edges of society, at times literally in the wild, at other times in a refurbished school bus that puts some of the Phish party buses I have been on to shame, he shows a man full of charismatic idiosyncrasies and dangerously controlling impulses. It is a far cry from his hero for all seasons in *The Lord of Rings* and a testament to his continued growth as an actor that he is able to pull this role off. I have always been captivated by these types of performances, when someone can lure you into feeling a certain way then completely pull the rug from under you and change how you perceive them.

These contrasts in character are evident early on, as we see Ben lead his family through a series of tasks that are designed to shape their physical and intellectual capabilities. His eldest son, Bodevan, played by George MacKay, must eat the heart out of deer he just killed in a scene somehow even more grotesque then the iconic one in *Indiana Jones and the Temple of Doom*. One of his daughters must pay the price for using the illegal word "interesting" by providing her analysis of *Lolita* before she can continue reading the book. The family ends a day that seems typical of these trials by having a jug-band jam out around the fire. Later they push on at Ben's urging during a rock climb in which one of the younger sons breaks his hands. Any collective malaise amongst the clan goes away, though, when Ben triumphantly declares they will still go to the funeral of his wife and their mother, Leslie (a haunting Trin Miller), whose suicide sets the main thrust of the plot in motion, as the family will be forced into conflict with The Man, with the Society they have learned to live apart from. As they are taken along this journey it was hard for me not to feel compelled with this way of living, outside the margins of the work-sleep-work routine that sometimes feels more like an imprisonment then a way to be a person who is truly free.

When the family makes it to the funeral, taking place in the traditionally staid and stilted environs of a church, they walk inside in full motley crew glory, taking their places in the pews in stride (similar to the end of the Oscar nominated Finnish short film *Do I Have to Take Care of Everything?*). Ben crashes the podium and tells everyone how Leslie really wanted to be laid to rest, deepening the rift he had with his father-in-law, Jack (Frank Langella), and leading his son who had earlier suffered the broken hand to move in with his grandfather. After orchestrating a failed operation to rescue said son that ends in a disastrous near death, he relents to giving Jack the custody of the rest of his family. Despite their objections to the "gross vulgarities" and the wasted space of the world in which they now are confined, Ben surrenders to the realities of the new situation, not wanting to put them in any more danger and surrendering to a safer, more traditional way of living in the world, symbolized by shaving his beard and looking generally forlorn and of a wayward, lost countenance. I was wondering if the movie would indeed end here and strangely submit to an orderly normalcy after flying so close to the sun. But it pivots back to its earlier manic throes, somewhat evoking *Little Miss Sunshine*, as the family comes together by rekindling the best parts of the spirit that had seemingly dissipated, by embracing the risk inherent in a life traversed with an open-mind, and re-harmonizing through their commensurate power of love for each other and for Leslie.

It is enough to raise my standards so that on subsequent reviews I am more critical of films that do not contain this much life, humor, drama, and truth. Until then, I'll have to re-watch *Captain Fantastic*, recommend it to everyone I talk with about movies, and think about other facets of the film I did not get to here, in the hopes that I'll get to them eventually.

What to Make of Robert Pattinson? (<u>Cosmopolis</u>)

I have only seen the actor known as Robert Douglas Thomas Pattinson act twice. Once as Cedric Diggory in <u>Harry Potter and the Goblet of Fire</u>, where I thought he gave a solid performance as the charming pretty boy without being too smug or too hollow. The other time as Eric Packer in <u>Cosmopolis</u>.

Visually, <u>Cosmopolis</u> is a gem, as constructed through the lens of David Cronenberg (helmer of <u>The History of Violence</u>, <u>Eastern Promises</u>, <u>The Fly</u> and others, and adapted from the Don DeLillo book of the same name). Pattinson, however, gives a performance that is stranger than the fake rapper Joaquin Phoenix portrayed in the bizarre yet definitely worth checking out <u>I'm Still Here</u>. It is basically a one-note acting job, albeit with a face of anguish at the end that slightly redeems the portrayal by showing us another layer to the character. The entire time Pattinson is basically squinting his eyes, looking downward, and slowly muttering opaque and derisive dialogue. It is a strange performance in a stranger movie. You can piece the story together of a young man who is paranoid about his bet on the yuan, the Chinese dollar, and about someone out there trying to kill him. The symbol of the rat as the new form of market control (or lack thereof, or something else about global economic affairs) is also woven throughout the film to give you something to hang onto. Still, I think it is an instance of Pattinson trying too hard to come off as weird and edgy and different from the Edward he plays in the <u>Twilight</u> movies, and in doing so makes a bizarre script that much more difficult to comprehend.

I actually understood <u>Cosmopolis</u> more when I contextualized it as a meta-movie about a movie star, with Pattinson as the avatar of the experience. In their lives away from the camera, we really have no idea who these people are, and attempt to decode the mysteries of their lives through the tabloids, interviews, and profiles in magazines, newspapers, and the web. They are worth millions, sleep with whomever they want ("when are we going to have sex again?" he asks a blonde in a bookstore), and ride around in slow convertibles as the world slowly revolves around them. They know there's something wrong, yet they end up finding out how that wrong is inextricably tied to their existence.

Here is Pattinson, acknowledging the misplaced adulation given to him for Twilight, and finding out he is the cause of his own misfortune. Here I am, trying to figure out if there is something more here, when there may be nothing more at all.

God Only Knows (<u>Love and Mercy</u>)

While watching <u>Love and Mercy</u>, the new Brian Wilson biopic, I couldn't shake Wilson's own take on the film, how he thought it was pretty good, but how he said what he went through was worse than what was depicted. On the surface this is somewhat obvious, of course the art is a reflection of reality and a warped one at that, but I think it is still a super-telling statement given how the intense events on screen unfold in a story that holds no punches and features an ensemble functioning as fluidly as all the instruments in the Pet Sounds orchestra.

Over the course of the narrative, we go back and forth between young, <u>Pet Sounds</u>-era Wilson and older, mis-diagnosed, reclusive Wilson, played by Paul Dano and John Cusack respectively. Having these two stories go in and out of another was an effective technique, as it allowed there to be two character arcs that merged in the end and formulated something that was greater than the sum of its parts.

The young Wilson arc gives us the fun misunderstood genius part of the story. In a pool party scene that sets the course of this story in motion, Wilson adamantly declares he wants to stay home and work on new music while the rest of the Beach Boys continue on the tour. The new music is in response to the waves the Beatles are sending out and becomes the instrumental harmonies on the landmark <u>Pet Sounds</u>. When the band comes back from the tour, though, they have a hard time meshing in with the new sound, which has been propelled by an energy that has long since drifted away from them and now soars in another orbit. Just how good is the new sound in concrete frames of comparison? "Better than Phil Spector" one session player tells Wilson to which he can only laugh. In our own lens it is as evident as the brilliance of the California sun and the sonic beauty of its waves, rushing and trickling over the shore in a naturally synchronous harmony. We can hear the flip side of this coin though, captured during a dinner scene when the clinks and clanks of everyone's silverware on their plates converges into a bone-jangling symphony rising in volume as an intolerable din. Despite all the success he has realized at this juncture, as "Good Vibrations" becomes the Beach Boys' best single to that point, you can feel the darkness creeping in.

The old Wilson seems to exist twenty or so years on, as a frazzled, heavily medicated, slightly paranoid, and oddly sweet man, with a hint of genius still rattling around in his brain. When you first see this character, after a few scenes with a Dano who more closely resembles the musician, with rounded face, big cheeks, and flickering eyes, you can't help but see John Cusack and give an inaudible sigh at the miscasting[32]. But Cusack portrays the character with such an indelible weirdness you can't help but want to figure this guy out and in so doing forget the dissimilar appearance. He meets and instantly falls for Melinda Ledbetter (played by Elizabeth Banks, who has never been better[33]), who embodies not only our curiosity for Wilson, who is he really and how can he love, but our hope that he can get out of the spell we see the musician falling into while watching the intersplicing narrative of his life as a younger man play out. She has to battle with Dr. Eugene Landy (played by Paul Giamatti, who delivers a raging bull of a performance as Wilson's malignant psychiatrist), a conflict that comes to a head in a brilliant burst of tension and release, as he flips out over a court summons and bangs on the windows of Ledbetter's office in a tantrum of all the misguidedly righteous ugliness he has displayed up until this point. He demands she open the door and any fear you have at what will happen if she does is diffused by how all his energy seems to release like a balloon when he sees this strong woman standing there and staring him down. Everyone is so damn good here I think it's folly to single any of them out, and how they meld together here is one of the greater joys I've had at the cinema in quite some time. It is a textbook example of the great back and forth

---

[32] John Cusack's one of those actors whom an inaudible sigh semi-regularly feels appropriate for.

[33] I'll see your Effie counter-argument, though.

actors can have with one another that amplifies their own performances and lifts the film as a whole.

But to get back to my initial diving off juncture for this piece (back into the deep end of the pool perhaps?), we see the young Wilson falling out of sorts with his bandmates, some of whom are his blood relatives, and notably how the strain with his father creates a deep pain within that he cannot reconcile with the music he so sublimely brings forth. We see the older Wilson being brainwashed by a man who wants to use someone else's genius for his own ends. Wilson is driven mad by those who cannot appreciate him and want to imprint their own meaning onto his life, cannot finish his masterpiece, and cannot be in love, until this final indignity is something he can only rectify by the same subconscious compass that let him bring such great music into the fray in the first place, now telling him he needs to listen to the thumping bass lines of his heart, even if they are on a take 32 so to say (who knew the final seconds of "Good Vibrations" took so long to perfect?). This is difficult stuff to go through no doubt, and one can only surmise from Wilson's review of his biopic that these rhythms are still playing out, still frenetically unresolved in his older age. Maybe the film only captures of the vibrations he was really feeling, God only knows what they were really like, but I am glad to have heard them, if only for a little while.

The Struggle Inside Llewyn Davis

On the surface, Inside Llewyn Davis is about a folk singer who plays in the West Village in the early 1960s. I've heard a lot of people comment on how dark the film is, but I do not see the film in the same light. Sure, Llewyn Davis does not realize the commercial success or notoriety of some of his peers, but that is besides the point. He is making his art, living out his ideals (however messy and convoluted they may become to perpetuate), and creating some undeniably poignant songs. Artists throughout history have been unsuccessful- Poe died on the streets a drunken, penniless man, Van Gogh in an asylum, without having sold a single painting in his life, while his paintings now go for hundreds of millions and people champion Poe as one of the fathers of American literature. None of this is to say the disconnect between artistic output, quality, and meaning and compensation is not a painful truth for many worthy artists. It most definitely is. Art though should be inherently priceless, created because its creator needs to bring it out into the world and give something of totally unique, uncompromising expression. That is what the Coen brothers do here, using stark images of open roads in the Midwest, swirling snow storms, an orange cat and its scrotum, stone walls, subway stations, and bathroom stalls to paint an immersive picture of a time in a place and its inhabitants, as if they too are saying, "there is some sense in tryin'."

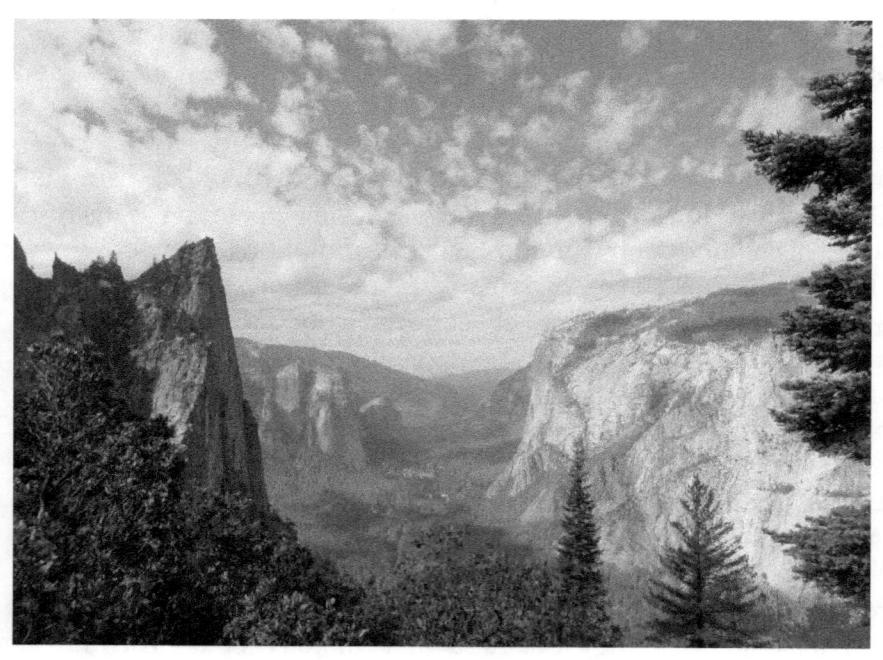

Yosemite National Park

The Name's Zimmer... Hans Zimmer

For a while a few years back, my default *Pandora* station was Hans Zimmer Radio. This was not out of any infatuation but because of some strange kink in the system that could not be changed. After a while I just let it stick. Hans Zimmer Radio was a solid way to start a new listening session; the first song was usually some inspirational piece or the chunk of score you would expect during a climactic sequence of a film.

Over his career, Zimmer has scored more than 100 movies. He is not as much a household as John Williams, but he has become about as surefire as you could expect from a composer. In recent years, Zimmer's music has helped set the tone of the Christopher Nolan Batman series. It is a dark, melodic sound that parallels the ups and downs of the caped crusader's journey.

How Zimmer amplifies Batman's trials and tribulations in The Dark Knight is the whipped cream on top of Nolan's rich chocolate mousse of a film. Zimmer's shaking, single note violin string is a simple line, yet ends up being the perfect way to signal the audience of the Joker's arrival, and sets a tense mood before the appearance of Heath Ledger in his tragic signature role. Usually you hear sirens on the street so you can pull over for the ambulance or the police. This composition is a warning of another variety.

It is no coincidence that this trick is derived from the one Williams pulled in Jaws to tell us the shark is coming. Nolan wanted the Joker to have the vibe of the monstrous great white because he comes out of nowhere and wreaks chaos on helpless victims. As iconic as Williams' Jaws theme is though, it did not come out of nowhere and actually has its roots in composer Antonin Dvorak's "Symphony No. 9: Movement IV: Allegro con fuoco." Zimmer's Joker theme, "Why So Serious," has its roots in the German band Kraftwerk[34], but could

---

[34] Thanks *Wikipedia* entry!

also be placed in the same tradition as frenetic violinists such as Niccolo Paganini.

In The Dark Knight Rises, Zimmer crafted the piece "Desha Basheraa" for the main villain, Bane. It is a war chant sung by Gotham's criminals as they rise up against the man who put them down ("What does that mean?" Bruce Wayne asks, to which Alfred responds, "rise."). Taking cues from the new-agey "world" school of music, Zimmer created the piece by splicing together thousands of voices from across the globe. The composer made a web site that allowed people to send in clips of their voices, which were subsequently mixed into the final cut of the chant. It is a furious anthem for the final film of the classic contemporary trilogy, and perhaps one of the defining pieces of a progressive classical virtuoso who has channeled the many sounds of the diverse languages of the world.

Rooney Mara is Awesome (<u>Ain't Them Bodies Saints</u>)

When I left work at a reasonable hour one night a few years ago I knew there was only one place I could go: the E. St. Landmark Theater to see the new film with Rooney Mara and Casey Affleck. Such is the magnetism of these actors.

<u>Ain't Them Bodies Saints</u> is the story of a couple broken apart by a shootout and the difficulty in the two getting back together. Mara plays Ruth Guthrie, who stays behind in Meridian, Texas, after Bob Muldoon (Affleck) turns himself in to the cops in the aftermath of the shootout. Guthrie lives with their daughter, Sylvie, who grows to be four by the time Muldoon escapes prison. Muldoon's escape is the main narrative thrust. Reuniting with Ruth drives the convict, as he highjacks his way back into town, ignores the warnings of Ruth's neighbor and old acquaintance Skerrit (played by Keith Carradine), and evades a group of hunters in a thrilling shootout in the dark, which was one of my favorite scenes of 2013[35], on his journey to the woman he loves.

That Mara and Affleck carry the film, with help from an able Carradine, is no surprise. They are two actors who are able to both sink into roles yet retain a charismatic individuality that can make you appreciate why we pay to see people portray people in the first place. My thoughts revolved around this paradox for much of the film. Was I compelled by how Mara embodied a woman who had lost the love of her life in the most gut-wrenching fashion, turned to raise a child on her own, and then struggled with the whirlwind of emotions caused by the imminence and impact of her lover's return? Or was I lost in those icy blue eyes, lured in by the hanging camerawork of cinematographer Bradford Young? Some of the shots

---

[35] Also making this 2013 list: <u>The Wolverine</u> train fight, James Franco's party in <u>This is the End</u>, and the zombies on the plane in <u>World War Z</u>.

of Mara sitting and zoning out seemed almost like a continuation of those in Steven Soderbergh's Side Effects, which may not be as problematic as that sounds, if only because of the ethereal mysteriousness these gazes convey, a priceless conveyance of a longer performance for Mara that stretches across these films and is her sort of artistic statement in a field populated by players all too willing to settle for the status quo of the safe limits of the movie star zone. In this way she sort of evokes James Dean, whose performances are larger than any of his films and are interconnected (the disillusioned teens in East of Eden and Rebel Without a Cause bleed into a symbol of American greed in Giant; for Mara, the jaded ex in The Social Network (a small but significant part in a defining film of the 21st century) evolves into the extremely jaded hell-bent cyberpunk in The Girl with the Dragon Tattoo, who descends into the seemingly over-medicated and/or seemingly working the system woman in Side Effects, who fades into a broken yet still persevering person in Ain't Them Bodies Saints[36], with a dash of the times thrown in (Dean's post-WWII teenage angst, Mara's millenial societal solipsism), and their inarguable sex appeal. Ultimately, I don't think it is any one of these single things that stand out more to me then another, but in the way the whole can be greater than the sum of its parts, in the way the whole can be flawed yet still strangely radiant, was the way in which Mara's performance resonates for me. It is a rare thing.

It is also a rare thing for Casey Affleck to be overshadowed. Affleck shows a quiet sort of command in the Bob Muldoon role. He strides into view on the fields to embrace Ruth, arm out to wrap her in a hug that he never really lets go of, even in prison, and even when Skerrit tells him there will be trouble if Muldoon ever tries to see his old flame, that type of serious, "I run this small town and you better watch yourself if you know what's good for you" kind of trouble. Affleck undercuts this unyielding confidence by inflecting the cadence of his Texas drawl with a pitch that is slightly higher than you would expect from either the character or Affleck himself. As the film progresses, the voice betrays a vulnerability in this tough,

---

[36] Consider the comparison just for this slice of films, as if Mara decided to retire immediately after this film, although working Carol into this list could be fun.

whip-strong drifter to the laws of a higher power, even if he can evade the ones on earth.

Citing the works of Flannery O'Connor and other prominent Southern fiction writers as influences, director David Lowery makes a bold full-length feature debut. He lets a fine cast go to work, and uses Young's cinematography, the lighting (the Texas sun hitting off small town houses in an Edward Hopper fashion), and score (flawlessly synchronized during the aforementioned shootout) to amplify his ensemble's performances. The frequent use of voiceovers, however, reflects the weaknesses that go along with the strengths of a richly poetic script, at times taking you out of the immediate moment, slowing down the narrative pace, and making you remember you are watching an artfully constructed story, instead of simply being able to lose yourself in the film's world[37]. Ben Foster's[38] performance also struck me as sort of bland, but that may be the result of him playing more of the straight man, and is certainly at least partly the result of being up against Mara, Affleck, and Carradine. Problems aside, Ain't Them Bodies Saints is worth seeing for the mesmerizing Mara and Affleck as envisaged through the lens of a promising new filmmaker[39].

---

[37] Which I have found to be a pretty good indicator of the film's quality, thinking too much about other things means the movie has failed to capture your attention
[38] Although he is excellent in the 2016 modern heist movie, *Hell or High Water*.
[39] In 2017 the Lowery, Mara, Affleck trio reunited for *A Ghost Story*, which I have recommended to people along with what I am sensing is a deal-breaking caveat of "there's a scene where Rooney Mara eats pie for like 10 minutes."

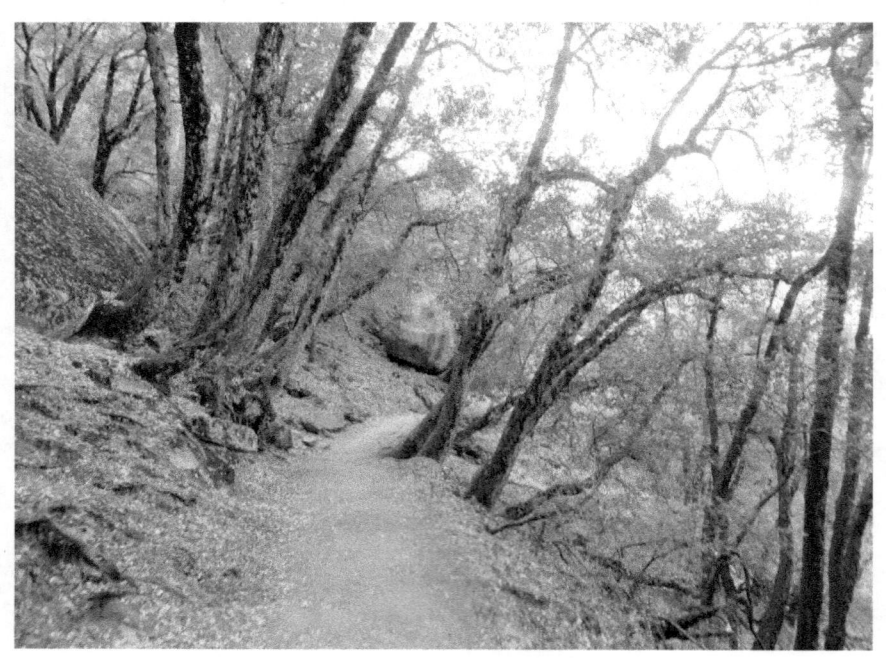

Yosemite National Park

Noteworthy Films from the 2017 Academy Awards

O.J.: Made in America

"This is why history is important. This is why documentary storytelling is important. It can take two decades to be able to look at that moment in a sober fashion and to look at how we got to that place."
-Ezra Edelman

It's kind of remarkable that the Academy can still screw up the Best Picture race, even though they expanded the field to have up to ten entries after *The Dark Knight* snub eight years ago. But the category still seems pegged for dramas, period pieces, and musicals, with *Arrival* really being the only exception to the rule here this year. The Academy's penchant for these types of films seems even more absurd when you consider that *O.J.: Made in America* was left out of the pool of best movies this year altogether. What Ezra Edelman has captured over seven-and-a-half hours is essential viewing, for understanding an important moment in our past and how it is still playing out today. It shows the O.J. Simpson trial as a symbolic battle in modern race relations, as something that went beyond the limits of a criminal trial, and in so doing went into a space where an immediate truth was sacrificed for something much larger and difficult to reckon with. It is also simply a fascinating character study that adds a new lens to the rise and fall of those who pursue the American dream, covering racial, political, social, judicial, sports, entertainment, and other spheres of society in an epic tableaux spanning 40 plus years.

The Salesman

"I believe that the similarities among the human beings on this earth and its various lands, and among its cultures and its faiths, far outweigh their differences."
-Asghar Farhadi

In the wake of the Muslim ban, the Iranian selection for Best Foreign Language film feels particularly important, especially since Asghar Farhadi boycotted the Oscar ceremony. What struck me most about the film, though, was how acutely normal the whole machinations of the plot were. A couple live in a city. They act in an adaptation of *Death of a Salesman*. They move into a new apartment. One day something terrible happens in the apartment. They grapple with the aftermath of the event. And the play goes on. The feeling may be akin to watching an Iranian adaptation of *Death of a Salesman*, you're watching a familiar work of art unfold in a way that still feels undeniably different and all the more rich for being so.

Manchester by the Sea

Similar to *The Salesman*, *Manchester by the Sea* transcends the specifics of the locale and serves as a gut-wrenching meditation on loss, family, and the ties that bind. Over the course of the film, there is an undercurrent theme of the desperation wrought about by depression, and is shown in scenes when Lee Chandler (Casey Affleck) explodes in fits of self-destructive, violent rage. It is the closest thing I've seen in recent years to a modern-day Marlon Brando-esque tour de force, and is something I think will echo on in years to come.

Reckoning with <u>12 Years a Slave</u>

No film I saw in 2013 had more hard truths about the world we live in, and the struggles of the past still playing out today, than Steve McQueen's adaptation of Solomon Northrup's memoirs. Physically and mentally brutal, with a sort of baroque, unrelenting intensity, <u>12 Years a Slave</u> is a haunting echo of a not so distant past; its villains, spouting obscenities and treating other human beings as livestock, reminding us of the evil we are all too capable of, and not too far removed from (about fifty years older than your one-hundred year old grandparent). The film is filled with horrible images and sequences that are as uncomfortable to watch as anything I have seen in some time; a slave merchant making a child jump as high as he can with his thighs to show the potential strapping "beast" he will become, a man hanging from a tree with his feet just close enough to the ground to be alive, spluttering blood and slowly dying, a woman taking so much abuse she would rather have her friend kill her than go on.

There is a dim flicker of hope amidst all this, marked in one scene by Brad Pitt's William Bass character listening to Northrup and spreading his story, and Northrup reuniting with his family, even though in the end you are left with a sobering realization that many were not rescued from this evil that existed for far too long (and many today are sadly still trapped in[40]). Even though this film won Best Picture, it exists beyond the coronation an award brings, as a vivid portal into the past, and a grimy, cracked mirror worth gazing into and pondering.

---

[40] Go to endslaverynow.org or similar sites for more information.

Cinematic Irony, Commerce, and Seduction in <u>The End of the Tour</u>

From the Editor: Last Friday, Brian Callahan, a reasonably productive, yet still leaving something to be desired, citizen of the U.S. of A., was last seen walking into the E. St. theater in Washington, D.C., to see the film *The End of the Tour*. I recall his state of emotions that morning at the office as being a conflated mixture of excitement and skepticism, as it were, his love of the late writer, David Foster Wallace, and the cinema presenting an impossible conflict of whether he could think through his emotions and rationalities and come to a tempered conclusion w/r/t the meaning and impact of the film, for his psyche and the collective psyche, the difference between the two, the convergence of the two, or lack thereof.

I write this as of late Wednesday night, having finally discovered Callahan's whereabouts in the George Washington university hospital and confirming with local authorities that he was the subject of a peculiar case down at the E St. theater, on E and 11th NW, in which they sent in a fire team to remove a gaunt man, eyeballs drooping down his face, saliva dripping off his lips and settling as a gloopy globule into his beard, pale as a ghost, hair matted and greasy and clumpy, near death and all adjoining formalities. Persons said Callahan had seen every showing of the film *The End of the Tour* since he first saw it on Friday the 7th, never questioned by patrons, and somewhat admired by the ushers, not just for the prodigious, marathon man movie watching rounds, but for being genuinely genial, evoking a level of sympathy that gave him enough temporary reverence to stay in the same seat until it got way too bad, said ushers admittedly realizing they should have done something, but not completely at fault due to their being shifted in and out of different theaters and thereby never gleaning the whole magnitude of the situation, plus having made a couple midnight showing announcements elsewhere, attending to other matters of the cinema and their lives and whatnot.

Reports are that all film reels of *The End of the Tour* have been transferred to the Landmark's Bethesda location, and that when the screen in E St.'s theater 4 annularized the images of the film into an incandescent shade of egg white hue, Callahan reluctantly submitted to movement, and unclenched his right fist enough to let go of a crumpled piece of paper with trace samples of the compounds found in exoebergian mitoxin[41].

Scrawled on these pieces of paper in a hand that devolved from lapidary stylistic flourishes to chalkboard screeching marks, were the different pieces of the puzzle he was trying to put together for his review of the film. As a jumping off point for the piece, instead of going the Mozart-Salieri *Amadeus*[42] route, or even with the controversy of the estate and people who knew Wallace versus David Lipsky[43] and the film, Callahan noted how Wallace often explored the nature of our relationship with viewing mass-produced images, most notably in his magnum opus, *Infinite Jest*, but in other works as well, particularly "E Unibus Pluram: Television and U.S. Fiction," and "The Suffering Channel." Thus it was ironic that these issues were now being brought to light in the same medium in which Wallace cautioned his audience about, from the standpoint of surface irony and re-appropriating the literary device into an arena in which it could only re-generate untruths about the surface, muddling our ideas on the depths of the truly beautiful, intangible aspects of the soul. He worries about people just seeing the film and not diving into the author's work and engaging through the printed page, more a

---

[41] Close cousin of doxycyclin hyclate.

[42] *Amadeus*. Year of the Chrysler minivan. AMLF, The Saul Zaentz company. Tom Hulce, F. Murray Abraham, Elizabeth Berridge, Roy Dotrice, Jeffrey Jones, Simon Callow, Cynthia Nixon; 70 mm; 160 min; color. Milos Forman's Best Picture winning biopic about the seminally precocious Wolfgang Amadeus Mozart, 18th century musical genius, and how the jealousy wrought by older, less naturally talented Antonio Salieri contributes to his downfall. VHS, DVD, Blu-Ray, streaming.

[43] Writer of *Although Of Course You End Up Becoming Yourself*, which chronicles the road trip conversation he conducted with Wallace and is the basis of the film.

direct pathway to the mind, citing a rich canon and use of time in so doing and not just relying on 100 minutes, but struggling with the unquestioned fact that deep down he really did enjoy this movie, as Jason Segel here was undeniably PSHian, for disappearing into the role, creating the illusion you are watching the person as he was, a realist portrayal, not theatrical, noting the qualities of his hypnotic eyes, looming large like saucers in the diner scene[44]. Jesse Eisenberg also as an audience avatar in the Lipsky part, smart, logical, fallible, above average but not idiosyncratically prodigious. And the crepuscular glow of the director's[45]camera as we go into and out of the flashback of the conversation on the road in the winter, imagining the field covered in snow in the spring, with its grass rippling like water, as a texture of the film to note, much as Wallace noted how fiction can create a texture, a feeling wrought through all the senses, when executed well.

And now there is the irony that Callahan is only able to explore these thoughts through my abstracted interpretation of his buttered popcorn notes, from beyond the pale, using the notes of a film to build out a review that reverse engineers the story back into the literary, for are we not still talking about film and if I have wandered has it not been within the confinement of the realm in which we take to be true in this context?

I wonder as to the points in which he crossed from skepticism and enjoyment to lethargy to waking sleep to coma, whether all of these elements appeared in some degree across all stages of this regression, whether micro- or macrocosmic and inextricably tied to the ineluctable doom of the enterprise he was exploring, whether it was saprophytic or intentionally paralytic. I wonder now, as he lies supine, breathing through tubes, heart palpitations rising and falling like rolling hills in the old country, whether seeing the film would affect my perspective of his perspective and irreparably alter the noble thoughts generated at the onset of this piece, from its true originator? Does he know that I know that he knows his true intent is a tightly wound ball of string, that only he can unravel and follow

---

[44] The seductive element, vis a vis.
[45] James Ponsoldt (1978-).

through the labyrinth of his mind? Who do I think I am that I can brush aside my own fallibility in this interpretation and push on, writing in words I think are my own?

If he ever awakes, I will ask him about the meaning he found in the commercial nexus spread throughout the film, references to McDonalds, Mountain Dew, Diet Coke, Taco Bell, Long John Silver's, Mall of America, *Broken Arrow*, *Magnum P.I.*, *Charlie's Angels*, *Happy Gilmore*, peanut M&Ms[46], Alanis Morissette, *Rolling Stone*, Pop Tarts. Until then, I hope these notes preserve a dim fragment of his conflicted thoughts and ease any concerns you may have as to his well-being.

---

[46] Unverified.

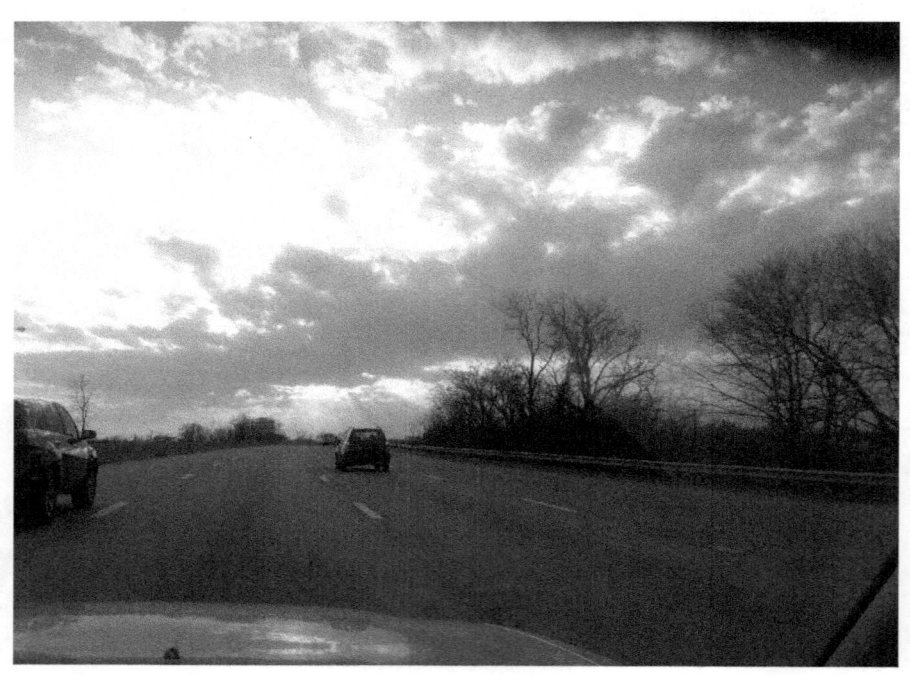

Act III: Of Heroes and Villains

Ext. Rooftop- Night

The That Person Was in Such-and-Such List

This is honestly an infinite list, but I thought it'd be fun to take a crack at it anyways. My criteria here is twofold- it has to be a person who at one point played a notable role (this accounts for the difference between recognizing a character actor versus someone who stole the show and left an indelible mark), and the movie you recognize the person in has to be noteworthy enough to merit caring (or else why get excited about it?). Bonus points for characters who are defined by one role so much you can't imagine seeing them in anything else until of course you do.

1. Richard Griffiths (Uncle Vernon in the *Harry Potter* series) is actually the Head Porter[47] in the Best-Picture winning *Chariots of Fire*.
2. Warwick Davis[48].
3. Before helping Tony solve all of his boring, 1st-world problems on *The Sopranos* as Dr. Melfi, Lorraine Bracco was Ray Liotta's squeeze in *Goodfellas*[49].
4. Bradley Whitford tries to hold Billy back in school in *Billy Madison*, kills Thor in *Cabin in the Woods*[50], and would have voted for a third Obama term in *Get Out*.
5. Diana Rigg hasn't just been the crafty matriarch of House Tyrell in *Game of Thrones*. She also goes ice-skating with James Bond in *On Her Majesty's Secret Service*.
6. Brad Dourif, who is the voice of Chucky and plays the lovable little guy in his human form, is also Doc Cochran in *Deadwood* and Billy Bibbit in *One Flew Over the Cuckoo's Nest*, which

---

[47] But I think this character would still scoff at a Platform 9 ¾ query.

[48] Okay I'm kind of cheating here, but making it through an entire book without an ode to the great Warwick Davis? Sacrilege! Also do you know Davis has been in the *Leprechaun* series, multiple *Star Wars* films, the *Harry Potter* movies, *Willow*, *Labyrinth*, *The Hitchhiker's Guide to the Galaxy*, and *Life's Too Short*? One of the great, underappreciated careers of all time.

[49] Shout out to Shimmy Raben for this one here. "The Ostrich" has long been a faithful reader of *PSH for President* and has probably liked more articles on Facebook then anyone I'm not related to.

[50] Chris Hemsworth's death scene is one of the most unintentionally funny scenes I've seen in a while. Bravo, Drew Goddard and Joss Whedon, bravo.

netted him a Best Supporting Actor Academy Award nomination.

7. Nestor Carbonnel played the mayor in *The Dark Knight*, as well as the ageless Richard in *Lost*.
8. Mandy Patinkin is the swashbuckling Inigo Montoya in *The Princess Bride* and the operative Saul Berenson in *Homeland*[51].
9. Remember Grand Moff Tarkin in *Star Wars*? He was played by Peter Cushing, who was also in several Hammer Films monster flicks, with the great Christopher Lee.
10. Seth Green (aka Scott Evil) is actually in the 2nd *X-files* episode and may or may not have really seen aliens[52].

11[53]. _____
12. _____
13. _____
14. _____
15. _____

---

[51] Thanks to Ken Beegan for this one.
[52] I believe him.
[53] Future reader contributions.

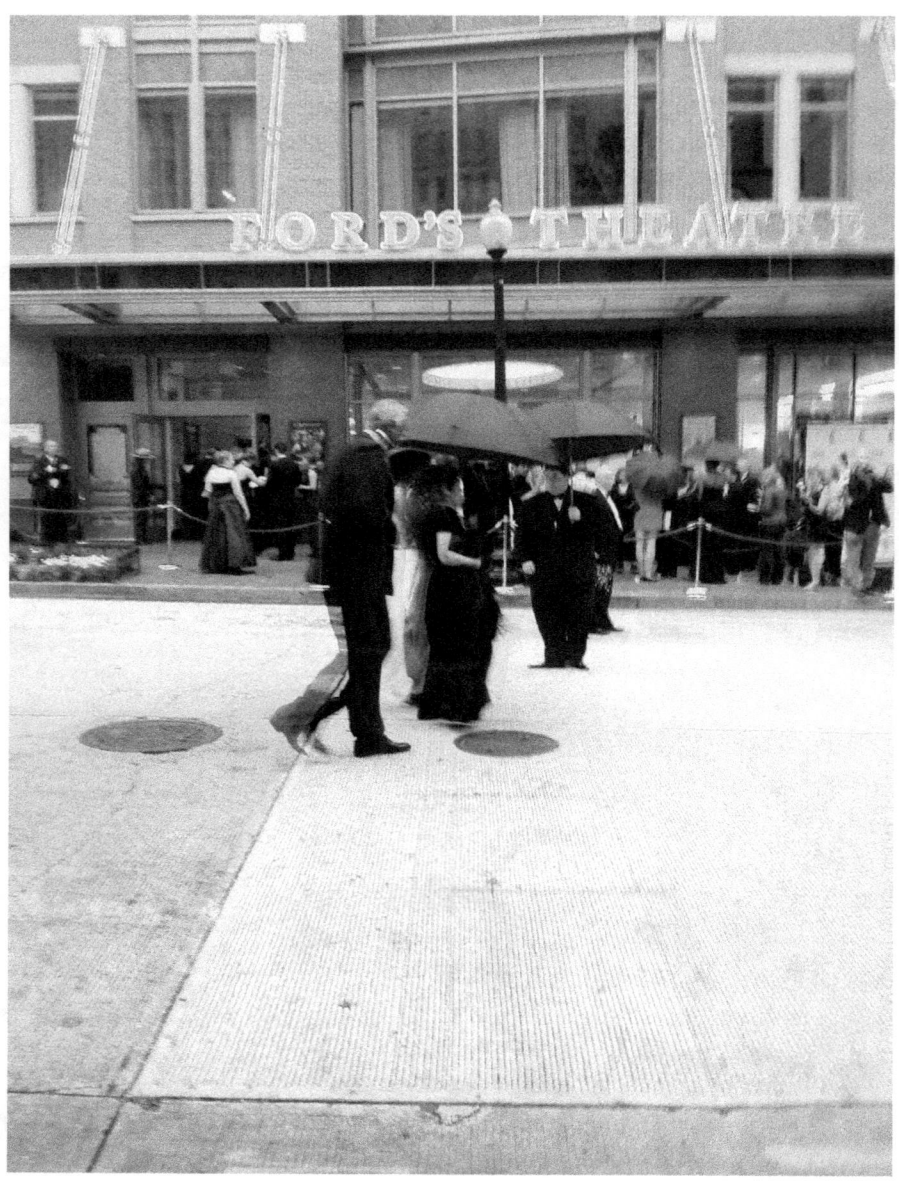

The great Bill Russell at a Ford's Theater gala in Washington, D.C.

PSH at the Barrymore on Broadway (<u>Death of a Salesman</u>)

"I have such thoughts, I have such strange thoughts."[54]

A few times in life you are afforded the opportunity to witness something grand. It is rare to experience the workings of a master in person, rarer still to see those ethereal qualities that make someone great at their craft come together in a sequence of transcendence.

In 2012 I saw Death of a Salesman with my uncle. We went to the play on Saturday night at the historic Barrymore theater on West 42nd street. The venue has played host to many great shows and performers over the years: Geoffrey Rush, David Mamet's <u>Speed-the-Plow</u>, Jessica Lange, Maggie Smith, Jessica Tandy, Katherine Hepburn, Anthony Perkins (aka the <u>Psycho</u>), Mia Farrow, Robert Duvall, Orson Welles' production of <u>Moby Dick</u>, Henry Fonda, Raymond Massey (James Dean's father in <u>East of Eden</u>), Marlon Brando in <u>A Streetcar Named Desire</u>, Gene Kelly, Fred Astaire, Laurence Olivier, and Ethel Barrymore, for whom the theater itself was named. Hoffman would be the latest and was a most able bearer of the theater's torch.

Elia Kazan put on the first production of <u>Death of a Salesman</u> in 1949 with Lee J. Cobb as protagonist Willy Loman. Over 60 years later, Mike Nichols (he of <u>The Graduate</u> and other classic films) directed Arthur Miller's Pulitzer Prize winning play. Hoffman stepped into the Loman role and was joined by a strong cast of Linda Emond as his wife, Andrew Garfield as his son Biff, Finn Witrock as his other son Happy, and John Glover as his brother Ben. Nichols set the play in its original time and place, a decision that gave me the feeling of stepping back into time and watching both an earlier era in

---

[54] Spoken by Hoffman as Willy Loman, written by Arthur Miller.

America as well as an homage to an artistic representation of that time. Over the years, other formidable actors have stepped into the Loman role. In the 1980's it was Dustin Hoffman. For the fiftieth anniversary in 1999 it was Brian Dennehy.

Although I could not travel back and see the other shows, I did not feel a great need to do so. For one, the production stayed true to the source, from the simple yet elegant set design (essentially consisting of Willy's home and office, as well as other places, like a hotel and restaurant) to the haunting flute melody that sounded at strategic intervals throughout the play. For another, Hoffman is so magnetic in the role that I could not have imagined anyone being better. My uncle said he would have wanted to see Cobb, who played Johnny Friendly in Kazan's On the Waterfront and who, according to legend, mumbled through rehearsals for days until he placed the script down, stood up, and disappeared into Willy Loman. In an interview for NPR, Hoffman said he did not believe the story, that Cobb was struggling and preparing for the role like anyone else would have done. Even in a small moment such as this, you get a good insight into how Hoffman comes off as the actor's actor. He does not mythologize Cobb but understands him through the same process he went through to prepare for the role. He is, in essence, understanding Cobb through the challenge of the Loman role, which he has become intimately familiar with by performing the role several times a week.

As difficult as Loman is for his family to understand, he must be equally difficult to play. He must be charming enough to win our affections yet pathetic enough to sell the frustration that comes out in his son Biff and epitomizes the hopeless quest that we all may realize we are on in this world, with its one-way path to the unknown end. He is a sympathetic loser who is driven mad by not seeing his hopes and dreams reflected in the mirror of his life. I found myself laughing at times at certain parts of the performance and then thinking about the sad undercurrent to those laughs. As much as I laughed when Loman slapped a woman's butt, this scene really shows that he is so ill-equipped to navigate the world that he blows his money for artificial pleasure while his loyal and doting wife waits for him to come home from an endless journey. When you see

Biff discover the prostitute in Loman's room during a college trip, the effect is devastating. The son that he sees himself in is horrified and disgusted with his father for living a lie. Willy cannot understand this as he thinks the world of Biff and has tried his best to help his son become the man he projects himself to be. Yet his son is so distraught by the incident that he no longer believes his father can convince the math teacher to give him the ability to make up for the failing mark through summer school. Biff accepts a downward course in his life because he knows he cannot change the past that has put him on this hopeless path.

Andrew Garfield held his own with Hoffman as Biff Loman. He ranged from the idealized All-American boy, full of youthful earnestness and naïveté, to a cynical adult, who is past his prime, desperate for work, and finally aware that he cannot hold himself to being the man his father projected himself onto many years ago. After reading the play, I got a sense of how difficult this role is, as the play works through the perspective of Loman and the memories and hallucinations that the present time creates for him. Garfield must appear as both the memory that Loman has as well as the conflicted self in the present that is difficult for Loman to comprehend. I saw Garfield after the play at a cool party full of New York City's elite (just kidding, I saw him outside the venue) and said I thought he would be great in the upcoming Amazing Spider-Man[55]. Garfield responded with an "I hope so," which I found somewhat odd because the performance is already captured and done with, but cool at the same time, as it revealed an earnestness and touch of humbleness for a rising star who probably received the loudest cheers out of any of the performers in the play, despite my best efforts to get a PSH chant going.

It is a testament to the actors in Nichols' production, as well as the timeless quality of Miller's material, that allowed this version of Death of a Salesman to soar. I am used to seeing Hoffman in film, a medium in which a director takes the best cuts of an actor and pieces them together to make one single stream of a performance. On stage an actor must reenact the performance for each show and does not

---

[55] Raise your hand if you remember Andrew Garfield was Spidey.

have the luxury of a retake. There is no camera or screen to hide behind and no completion of a scene until the run of a show ends. It gives the experience a natural quality that is sadly fading away from cinema with the advent of increasingly powerful technologies that may be well used in some hands or soul-crushing and commoditized in others. For one night on Broadway, though, Hoffman was as magnificent as I hoped he would be. He made Willy Loman real[56].

---

[56] *Editor's Note:* This was a tough piece to write. The performance was so mind-boggling good that I cannot really comprehend it, cannot truly express what it was like to see the master in person. Film offers repeat viewings, the theater gives you one.

Seeking A Most Wanted Man

"I have broken all the rules."

And then some. It is a treat watching Philip Seymour Hoffman in one of his final bows[57], showing off everything that made him such a great actor and artist who will live on for generations to come. The way he walks, talks, breathes, reacts, brings to life a sea of demons lapping beneath a façade of calm, razor focus is a sight to behold.

As Günther Bachmann, Hoffman is the lead of a German intelligence unit stationed in modern-day Hamburg. When a mysterious man from Chechnya who has a claim to a significant sum of money and is suspected of being involved in terrorist activities arrives in the city, Bachmann finds out where the money is going and decides on helping the man in the hopes of catching a bigger fish. But dealing with interference from the U.S. and Germany's higher-level intelligence becomes a thorn in this mission. I won't spoil the plot for you, partly out of an inability to completely retell the intricacies of this John Le Carre adaptation[58] in a way that does justice to the work, but also partly because Hoffman's layered performance helps unravel this spool.

But how do you untangle this performance? Is it in the gait of his stride as he confronts Willem Dafoe's banker? Or the pained guise he wears when he cannot accept the mistakes he's made that cost innocent lives? So much of what makes Hoffman great is on display here, how he melds all the verbal, physical ticks into another being, and vanishes before your eyes into something else. In A Most Wanted Man, Hoffman carries the weight of so many failures, of ~~spies who could not find the ri~~ght piece of intelligence at the right

[57] The split third act of The Hunger Games, the John Slattery film God's Pocket, and the unreleased pilot of Happyish being the others

[58] Screenplay by Andrew Bovell. Another recommended Le Carre' adaptation is the 2011 film version of Tinker Tailor Soldier Spy, which features Gary Oldman at his finest.

time, of groups working toward the same end being unable to work together, of people disconnected with others. He makes you consider so much, about the choices and consequences made not only in the setting of the film, but in other situations that could very well have taken place across the ages. In this sense, the essence of his character bleeds out from the cinematic confines, a ghost permeating into the realities of our world.

Augmenting this Hoffman coda are fine performances from Robin Wright, Rachel McAdams, Willem Dafoe, Nina Hoss, Grigoriy Dobrygin, and Daniel Bruhl (the Nazi movie star in Inglourious Basterds), along with compelling direction from Anton Corbijn, who makes his feature film debut in an admirable style that lets the actors dive into the personas and motives of their characters amidst a setting marked by a dark, noir-esque cityscape. The plot offers no easy answers and inverts conventional cat and mouse tropes, the hunt is the thing, wherein to catch the conscience of a king…

Exploring the Work of Philip Seymour Hoffman through his Collaboration with Paul Thomas Anderson

"Man is not an animal."[59]

In a January 2015 interview with Marc Maron, director Paul Thomas Anderson describes the time he watched Philip Seymour Hoffman in Scent of a Woman as a love at first sight kind of moment. "I knew he was for me, and I was for him," he said, couching the revelation in terms of an unsurprising surprise that his definitive character actor/leading man would not be a traditional Cary Grant archetype. These heartfelt sentiments are not what you normally hear when learning about collaborators but they make sense when you inspect the union a little more closely. What keeps bands together? What keeps players on the same team with one another over the course of long careers? What makes someone want to be someone's editor? The specifics of a given institution may decide all that to a certain degree, but at the end of the day it comes down to people being inspired enough by one another to make a commitment with one another in their chosen field. It may not always be love in the forms that we know it- platonic, sexual, what have you- but with certain partnerships love is undeniably a good place to start.

It is hard for me to think of Hoffman and Anderson as distinct from one another, as they seem so inextricably tied together in their work that it seems folly to split the two apart. To me, Hoffman feels like the embodied spirit of Anderson's films, in all their dark, strange, tragicomic, twisted, and beauteous glory. And, on the converse, Anderson's films feel like they are directed by someone who would be like Hoffman, the consummate professional, probing into the strange recesses of the human psyche, exploring the shadowed

---

[59] From *The Master*, written and directed by Paul Thomas Anderson.

animus of society, and always doing so in an irreverent, technically brilliant, showman-like yet sublime manner.

In taking a through line across their collaborations you can not only magnify elements of the films that make them a special part of the late twentieth century and early twenty-first century American film canon, you can see the microcosms of different character types Hoffman employed throughout his career that help illuminate his style and power as an actor. Even though the focus here is on Hoffman, it is still hard to not think about the man behind the camera, as his choices and technique influenced or at the least guided the actor in a fortuitous direction. He is there even if you cannot see him.

It is fitting that The Master was the pair's last collaboration, as it showcases the two artists at the height of their powers. Whether you end up interpreting the film as expressing the sort of platonic love that can exist between two people, a statement on power and submission, or as a film saying something else completely, it is hard to argue against the sheer virtuosity on display from the director, the lead actors, and everyone else involved in the project. For Hoffman, it is a culmination of his talents as an actor on screen, as his Lancaster Dodd is a turbulent mix of joy, sadness, excitement, anger, confidence, fear, self-assurance, self-loathing, repression, charisma, cunning, and humor, characteristics applied from his various character types across his career but never so sublimely melded as they are here.

But how did he get to such great heights? Tracking Hoffman's work in Anderson's films provides a neat evolutionary line for the actor, as he goes from the cocksure young gambler in Sydney[60] to the full realization of the magnetic cult leader in The Master, from a small part you might miss due to how it blends into the environment, to a seminal leading role that you can't look away from or stop thinking about. From this point A to point B the route is as off-kilter as you would expect, as Hoffman and Anderson zig-zag between characters, settings, conflicts, and other elements. By looking at each of the films in which Hoffman and Anderson collaborated on, you can see

---

[60] Released as Hard Eight, but referred to by its original title here.

how they played off each other and forged unique, layered, complex, meaningful, and resonant creations.

In Sydney, Hoffman's first collaboration with Anderson, Hoffman is credited as "Young Guy at the Craps table." Despite being in only one scene here, you can see the seeds of greatness begin to sprout. Hoffman makes what could have been a throwaway role his own, weirdly maniacal one, and when he taunts Philip Baker Hall, he shows he can hang with the big boys. It is a brief appearance, but even in the limited duration, Hoffman imbues the character with a fiery energy that can be acutely seen in his star-is-born turn in Scent of a Woman. He is not as far along in his maturity as an actor in Sydney (and is also somewhat constrained by what the role and the film asks for), but Hoffman's exuberance in the presence of a mature father figure reflects a need to impress that is something we all probably succumb to at some point or another in our lives. His moment here is brief and staged within the larger casino world we see in other parts over the course of the film, but he still stands out and makes his first mark in Paul Thomas Anderson's filmic universe.

Although he was a man of the theater, a forum in which it helps to have more physical, externalized expressions on display, Hoffman was equally at ease on the silver screen, at home with various camera deployments, and able to portray the subtlest of gestures, offering an invitation into the cauldron of thoughts boiling beneath the surface. In Boogie Nights, Hoffman's Scotty J harbors feelings for Mark Walhberg's Dirk Diggler that percolate throughout the film and culminate in the famous "can I kiss you? Can I kiss you on the mouth?" scene, which is just about as devastatingly tragic of a sequence you will see on film. How Hoffman gets us to this point shows his early considerable prodigiousness as an actor. His entrance into the film is classic in how he bounces onto the screen, seemingly filled with sunshine and inquiring with his first lines, "is she alright?" of a woman's limp body, which has a face caked in blood, being carried by two guys out of the party. On the surface he seems oblivious to what's going on, and that may truly be the case, but he is also failing to recognize what is really happening around him. Later at a scene in the club, Scotty is introduced to a woman and ignores her a few times before giving into the social expectations of the situation. This may have been Anderson's direction here, but it is a subtle cue to the character's sexuality that adds to the portrayal's realism. Further yet, the look of restrained awe he gives Diggler in his first sex scene also contributes to this portrait of a character struggling with who he is. The New Year's Eve hookup attempt, then, is made all the more devastating by how excited Scotty J is and how we may even be rooting for him to succeed, even though we are fairly certain he will fail.

Even though Philip Seymour Hoffman may have made his mark playing folks out of left field, he was still able to reel it all in and play simply good people. Nowhere is this more evident then in his turn as Phil Parma in Anderson's neo-Valley epic Magnolia. As Parma, amidst Anderson's swirling cavalcade of raining frogs, whiz kids, sex fiends, and fractured vocal orchestras, you see Hoffman as a truly nice person, without the shades of gray you often find in his other performances. You don't know much about Parma other than his being a nurse for Earl Partridge (Jason Robards in his final film role) and, as such, he doesn't need much reconciliation at film's end. What he does is serve as a center of moral gravity, simply being there for Partridge and helping this ailing man on his deathbed forge one final connection with his son. In keeping with Hoffman's penchant for complexity, there are hints of weirdness in the character, but all in all he's a decent fellow, with his own idiosyncrasies, who gives you hope there are others out there like him somewhere along life's highway.

The flip side to this coin can be found in Anderson's black romantic comedy, Punch Drunk Love, in which Hoffman plays the seedy, small-time villain Dean Trumbull, the mattress man/phone sex scammer and ringleader. Although he only has three scenes, Hoffman is a ball of fire in all of them. You can tell he and Anderson are having some fun here, from the wild head of hair Hoffman sports to the vocal explosion on the other end of the line when Adam Sandler's Barry Egan calls him out for the scam and the muggings. It is riveting theater that you wish lasted longer (yet might be perfect in its brevity), seeing Hoffman so unhinged and completely reveling in the sliminess of his character, a far cry from his Phil Parma of a few years earlier, and when Barry finally confronts the mattress man in person, the showdown is classic, Sandler and Hoffman in a staredown, neither character nor actor backing away from the challenge. Although one of his smaller roles in a Paul Thomas Anderson film, Hoffman's Trumbell is essential viewing for its sheer awesomeness and as testament to the range he had as an actor.

*

On the surface of The Master, there are the usual suspects of the traditional hero's journey storytelling structure, represented by the antihero's odyssey to find himself after a war and how the people he meets set a course for his life. But beyond being an examination of the relationship of two men of polar opposites, The Master has no clear conclusion, takeaway, or message.

I think you can view the film as a dark mirror that changes depending on your perspective at the time of viewing. It is a layered work of art that is filled with different elements you may focus in on, whether it's the sublime acting of the leads[61], the rich 70MM cinematography, how the scenes are meticulously arranged with symbols hearkening to the composition of still-life paintings, the allusions to religion, cults, war, alcoholism, and homosexuality, and other dynamically arrayed pieces that form a whole greater than the sum of its parts. How you parse out the symbols of different shots, interpret the motives of the characters and the nuances to their relationships, think about the Cause for how real world religions attempt to explain the unexplainable and provide a moral code, really makes all the difference[62]. I think of The Master as a

---

[61] Hoffman, Joaquin Phoenix, and Amy Adams, along with Christopher Evan Welch, Jesse Plemons, and Laura Dern.

[62] In my perspective, I see The Master as a cinematic flow of the following: Sex as fleeting as the sand sculpture of a woman on the beach facing the tides. The churning water left in the wake of Freddie Quell's Navy boat and Lancaster Dodd's Alethia as a chaotic wake frothing out of the stillness of a world. Repeating the answers to deeply personal questions as a way to burn the emotions that come with this interrogative process into your subconsciousness. The motorcycle as harnessing a human-made mechanical creation in a controlled manner (riding to a point on the horizon and returning) and an uncontrolled

deconstructionist epic, about things coming apart and never reconnecting, about film's failure to serve as a didactic tool for good[63], and about the United State's hypocrisy in making people risk their lives in war and then not fully taking care of them when they come home.

All this is wrapped up in a film that is the culmination of Hoffman's partnership with Anderson, and represents the actor at the height of his powers. Hoffman is equal parts the raging animal that Phoenix is here, raging against those who question anything about the Cause, testing and questioning Phoenix's Freddie Quell to the point where it feels like torture, and threatening Quell in their final encounter, yet also coming off as a dignified, civilized individual through his refined, stately manner of being, how he elegantly handles himself, almost floating off the floor instead of walking, and how he gives off a seductive calmness and sense of refined righteousness in his interactions with people, in one-on-one conversations and in front of crowds, that would probably resonate for millions of people willing to believe in what he is preaching. Maybe, in a way similar to how Anderson's subsequent film, Inherent Vice, is about the formidable post-modern author Thomas Pynchon, The Master is about Philip Seymour Hoffman. Who else could embody so much, treat all his roles with equal care and dignity, exude the repressed animalistic tendencies in the shell of a man, and be worthy of the title of this film?

*

There is a lot more to be said about Paul Thomas Anderson himself, how his technical virtuosity and singular style recalls masters like Terrance Malick, Robert Altman, Stanley Kubrick, Robert Downey,

---

manner (riding into the point on the horizon). Peggy finding meaning in her husband's creation but less so in the person himself. The Cause as Dodd's self-help guide for the living, changing and evolving as he studies Quell and encounters non-believers, and develops his updated take on the life philosophy, which supersedes the original version and open's a Pandora's box of contradictions.

[63] If you take The Cause to be a stand-in for film, an abstract homage to Stanley Kubrick's black monolith in 2001: A Space Odyssey, and agree with the perspective of characters who find it foolish.

Martin Scorsese and other great directors through the ages, so I will not expound too much on that here. But I will take a moment to harp on There Will Be Blood, which is the film that really turned me on to Anderson and, incidentally, the only one released in Hoffman's lifetime that he did not appear in. What attracted me to the film when I first saw it, and what has kept me riveted ever since, was its unflinchingly dark portrayal of the world as a place where capitalism corrupted and beat down religion with bowling pins, marked by hypnotic shots of the American west, oil spouting like a volcano into the big blue sky, fire raging over a landscape already scorched by the sun, Johnny Greenwood's violent, thrashing score of piercing violin and rickety-bridge percussion, and a malevolent businessman, played with a wicked, theatrical glee by Daniel-Day Lewis, trampling over everyone and everything in his path. I saw this film during my sophomore year of college, and can still vividly remember going into this movie at the time[64] and going out a changed soul, thrilled by the possibility of the cinema and taking refuge in this shadowed corner of the universe. In a way, Anderson's films are shelters for that strange part of your subconscious you don't know what to do with, and for a while Philip Seymour Hoffman was a vessel that went through these worlds, reporting back on our fallacies and virtues with a marvelous grace. Although he is gone from us in a physical living sense, his spirit lives on not only in these films and the others he made throughout his career, but in the work of his colleagues like Paul Thomas Anderson and in those who were inspired by his art.

In Inherent Vice, the first film Anderson released after Hoffman's death, there are no clear corollaries to draw between the characters and the plot depicted on the screen and whatever Anderson must have been feeling at the loss of his dear friend. The film is decidedly unclear, the first Pynchon adaptation to make it to the screen, and puts you in the shoes of the lead detective played by Joaquin

---

[64] I saw this film in Cambridge, Massachusetts at a super groovy movie theater near my favorite restaurant of all-time, the Border Café. It is no longer in business but there are still paintings of Charlie Chaplin and Marilyn Monroe outside the spot where it once operated (this became an obvious choice for the cover). If there's ever a Boston film museum it should be housed in this spot (I'm looking at you Ben Affleck and Matt Damon!).

Phoenix, as he wades through the haze of reactionary, silent majority politics in this 1970s dark dramedy inspired by Altman's <u>A Long Goodbye</u>, Roman Polanski's <u>Chinatown</u> and other similar films of the film noir genre. Maybe it is as if Anderson himself is wandering through the smoke of a wreckage, wondering where to turn and look for answers, finding nothing and knowing there is nothing that can reconcile anything that has happened. It is the sort of mystery you can't really figure out, and, when considering the relationship he had with Hoffman, you can understand why nothing logical would present itself.

In a way, I am performing a similar role to Anderson here, albeit one step further removed, sleuthing through this cinema in order to find a harmony among the disparate parts, reaching for connections I think are there and hoping the journey will mean something, while remaining befuddled at the mystery of it all. I can write about what I saw in these films, what I think about them now, and what I think is worth imparting to you for some measure of posterity and maybe even inspiration, but they are a dim reflection of the greatness that once was, a light turned to a shadow slowly receding behind the curtains, and into the dark.

Why Do We Fall? (<u>The Dark Knight Rises</u>)

We are often in awe of the spectacles of Hollywood. The larger than life figures who cannot be real. The idealized moments that can only happen in the movies. Toward the end of <u>The Dark Knight Rises,</u> Batman (Christian Bale) reminds police commissioner Jim Gordon (Gary Oldman) how you can be a hero by putting a coat on a frightened child. You do not have to dress up, train in the League of Shadows, spend a fortune on cutting-edge technology, or fight terrorists. You can be a better person in the little moments. By looking out for the young, old, poor, and handicapped. By picking up a piece of litter in the street. By being a harmonious part of a community.

Although he has a knack for the theatrics, director Christopher Nolan is equally adept with depicting smaller, more intimate moments. In <u>The Dark Knight Rises,</u> these sequences are often dialogues between two characters that give us insight into the larger themes of the film and of The Dark Knight trilogy. Batman's final exchange with Gordon is one of those scenes because it illuminates Batman's greater purpose – Batman knows that despite his power, despite his ability to defeat the city's worst criminals, he is just one man. He needs others to help, even if it's in the smallest of ways. The symbol of Batman can only endure through the actions of the people who inherit the city he protected.

Bruce Wayne expresses this idea of Batman as a symbol in a conversation with Alfred in <u>Batman Begins.</u> His fight against crime must be larger than life to improve the quality of life for millions of people.

The trials and tribulations of <u>The Dark Knight </u>are a direct challenge to the need for a Batman. The billionaire orphan playboy states how "Batman has no limits." The Joker makes Batman take a deep look into oblivion, where "everything burns." As much as the Joker brings Harvey Dent down, he pushes Batman to the edge of his strict moral code, and causes him to abandon his post and become a fugitive from the law.

To protect his city as it faces an apocalypse in <u>The Dark Knight Rises,</u> Wayne must embody the best of what he believes Batman to be, even if he is past his prime. Wayne's physical failings are evident throughout the beginning of the film. Catwoman (Anne Hathaway) kicks away his stick. He hobbles to a charity dance. A doctor says he is not fit for heli-skiing because there is no cartilage in his legs.

None of this is lost on the guardian of Gotham's guardian, Bruce Wayne's butler, Alfred Pennyworth (Michael Caine). Alfred forces Wayne to think about whether Batman's return is a sound idea. He recommends Wayne think about the decision logically. Is Bruce Wayne someone who thinks Batman can come back or is Batman someone who can actually come back? It is an emotional climax for the journey these two men have taken. Alfred realizes he was an accomplice to the beast that he now believes should not exist. Wayne feels betrayed from the closest parental figure he has ever had. The two disagree, each clinging stubbornly to his own ideas, and part ways.

Soon after this exchange, Bane (Tom Hardy) breaks Batman's spine and Bruce Wayne finds himself in a prison that is notorious for offering its prisoners a false sense of hope. Wayne makes two attempts of climbing out of the vertical tunnel and into the light. On his first try he goes on pure adrenaline from the recovery of the Bane injury. On the second, he is fueled by anger. On his third he goes without the rope that is commonly used by the prisoners as an aid.

We are all in that prison now. We see and hear signs of hope but they do not seem real, they are out of reach, and cannot undo the horrors that have given us so much pain. After Bruce Wayne falls on the second effort, he envisions his father, who is extending a hand as a lift out of the darkness on the bottom of a well. "Why do we fall?" he asks. How do you live out the answer to that question?

Bruce Wayne climbs because of his father and mother, because of Rachel, because he accepts the responsibility to be the symbol of good that these brave people inspired him to be. He leaps with the strength of the people whom he has embraced. He fights Bane again with the strength of an entire population.

The Dark Knight is larger than life when his positive qualities come out of the screen and into us. He shows how you can use the energy of those who are no longer with us to combat evil and foster peace.

In loving memory:

Jonathan T. Blunk
Alexander J. Boik
Jesse E. Childress
Gordon W. Cowden
Jessica N. Ghawi
John T. Larimer
Matthew R. McQuinn
Micayla C. Medek
Veronica Moser-Sullivan
Alex M. Sullivan
Alexander C. Teves
Rebecca Ann Wingo

And to all others who have lost their lives to senseless violence

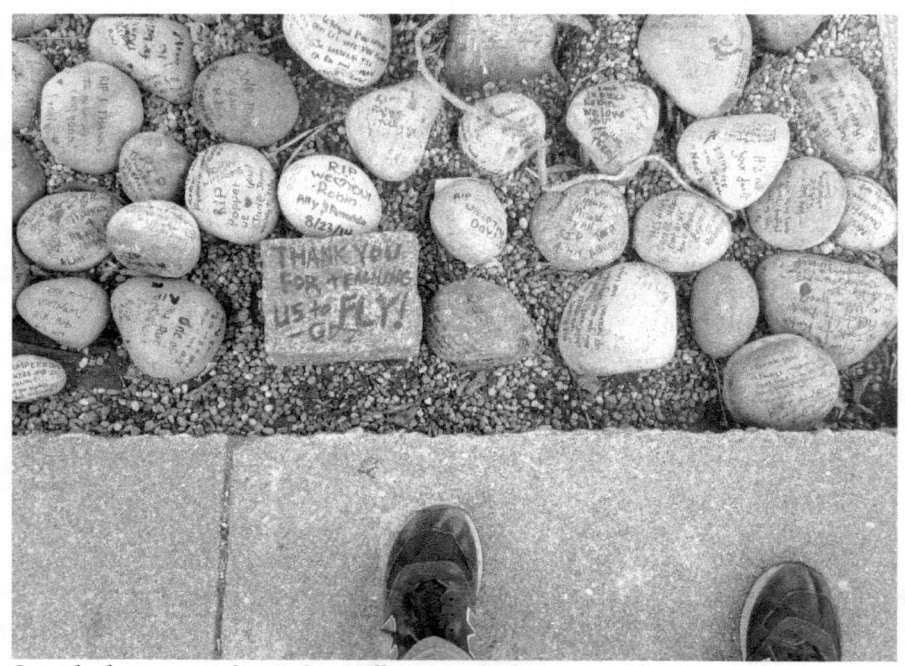

Outside the memorial to Robin Williams at the house used for <u>Mrs. Doubtfire</u> in San Francisco.

Epilogue

"So yo then man what's *your* story?"
- David Foster Wallace, *Infinite Jest*

Around the time of New Year's 2016 I went on two long city walks, one with my brother in Boston and the other with my uncle in New York. The Boston walk was in tribute to the late writer David Foster Wallace by way of various settings in *Infinite Jest*. The New York walk was deemed the "PSH Reality Tour" and was structured around the path Philip Seymour Hoffman took on his final night. There was something cathartic for me about getting out of the mental spaces these people occupied in my brain, and into their worlds, both real and imagined.

Over six years ago now I went on a walking tour of haunted New Orleans. Our tour guide led us past the above-ground graves in the Garden District, past houses with walls that could literally talk if you'd question them, past famed vampire novelist Anne Rice's abode, at one point recalling a story of how Nicolas Cage had joined her tour and inquired as to the haunted reputation of the mansion he had moved into. What seemed most important to her, though, was the memories of friends who had passed during Hurricane Katrina, people whose souls still seemed to linger on those streets, whose presence you could still feel.

There is an acute difference to walking a city in the winter. Even the generally warm ones like Los Angeles have a different feeling to them, in certain parts after hours, with businesses shutting down and the lights overhead slowly turning off, in places that are empty save for sidewalks and streets, office building edifices and your own thoughts. Even when you are not directly in these places you can

113

sense the night coming towards you, creeping along like shadows as the day breaks and darkness comes earlier then you'd like. The day in Boston was cold and overcast and the evening came sooner than we would have liked.

To navigate our course on the Boston walk, I found a website called *Infinite Atlas*, which plotted out all the points of events that took place in *Infinite Jest*. There were a lot of places in the greater Boston area, even one so far into the suburbs as the town where we went to high school, Acton. I wondered about Wallace briefly considering Acton at the edge of his story, a coordinate on the edge of a sprawling map that was so small it could fall off without notice, a brief flicker in the galactic storm of his cranial universe as perhaps my only connection to the writer. I figured we could hit a few of the places of the book in Cambridge and the Kendall MIT area, perhaps venturing out to the Brighton area to the halfway home that inspired the one in the story.

The night before we went on the walk in Boston there was a snow and ice storm that left the car we were taking encased in a sheet of thick ice. Before we left for Boston, we spent what must have been at least an hour breaking off big frozen chunks of the ice and scraping off the remaining layer. I remember banging my fist in certain parts of the coating because you couldn't get at it any other way. There was something satisfying about this process, metaphors of breaking the shell, or shedding a skin notwithstanding. My brother made the drive into the city, both of us relishing the trip as a release from lingering holiday tensions and small town blues.

When we got to Alewife we took the T train up to Harvard Square, where we got off to explore the stops in downtown Cambridge. The first stop was our favorite Mexican restaurant, the Border Café', where we feasted on the Camptown shrimp, chips, and quesadillas. This had nothing to do with *Infinite Jest*, but may have been the most essential stop on our journey. Afterwards, we went to an Au bon Pain, which was mentioned in the book as a place where "70s-era guys in old wool ponchos play chess," although we didn't see any that fit the description that day, and were mostly there for the coffee. When we walked back outside we were again in an important place of the story, where yrstruly, Bobby C, Poor Tony Krause, DesMonts, and Pointgrave roam in their ever-present fictive realm, stealing hearts and thinking about drugs.

On the PSH Reality Tour less than a week later, I imagined a world where Hoffman was still taking that final walk of his. Some theory goes that history is always happening, the past is still being played out, or maybe time as we know it – the past, present, and future – are all part of the same circular continuum. In this sense, Hoffman will still be going in and out of his apartment, still taking out too much cash from the grocery market ATM, still getting a cheeseburger and cherry coke from Automatic Slim's. All of his life's moments could be playing again on an infinite loop, the big ones and the small, or at least the ones captured on film and ably summoned by the insertion of a disc into a drive or the click of a button on an ethereal webpage.

In *Infinite Jest*, there is a movie called the Entertainment that is said to be so hypnotic it drives anyone who watches it into a vegetative stupor, ultimately killing them because they can't peel themselves away from it into doing something that will be less pleasing. The Entertainment's viewers must watch it because to stop watching would make them aware of their now even more unfulfilling lives, but by continuing to watch they stop eating, stop drinking, stop basically doing the things you need to do to live. It's a commentary on our own increasingly reliant dependence on filmic medium, sure, but it also sounds like a drug people would like to take if they knew they could be pulled from the brink before falling in. The Entertainment is a major entity in *Infinite Jest*, looming over the proceedings almost like a more intangible, trickster sort of Sauron. There weren't really any signifiers of its presence on our urban hike through Boston, although maybe we just didn't notice.

Without going into superlatives about the size of *Infinite Jest*, the best way I could describe its considerable length is that we spent a day walking around a city and only hit on a few of its sentences, maybe .1% of the contents. So if you spent a 100 days just hitting up Infinite Jest landmarks you'd get to a solid 1%, and only be 99,900 days away from hitting them all[65].

---

[65] Obligatory honorary footnote – not ALL the book is a stream of locale

The decimal points we marked off that day also included the Sheraton Commander hotel, referenced as a place where there had been a press conference gone awry (the hotel in this sense is already framed in the past in the book), the American Repertory theater, mentioned as a place where a weed addict's ex once performed (small, secondary character association detail checked-off), the Bow and Arrow pub (also the site of the iconic "you like apples?!" scene from *Good Will Hunting*), and Ryle's Jazz club (its closure making us wade farther into the night to find a place to grab a beer). Not counting Ryles, which we passed later in the evening on our return leg, the route took us on a winding sort of loop through Harvard Square, not too dissimilar from the shape a shoelace might fall into if you dropped it. We walked along the old campus quads, past an outdoor bookstore, and past a graveyard, I think.

When we had our fill, we went a few stops up to Kendall-M.I.T. and explored the M.I.T campus for a bit, as it features prominently in Wallace's book as the place where we first learn of the mysterious Madame Psychosis, where James Incandenza mastered optical physics, and where the Militant Grammarians of Massachusetts held a convention that sparked the infamous language riots of B.S. 1997. My brother and I both commented on how the place made you feel smarter, whether through the brainwaves floating in the environs, the intellectual karma, or how the more literal signage, structural shapes of the buildings, and sculptures scattered through the grounds seem to spark neurons in the mental pathways (you can walk inside a sculpture of a large brain for Pete's sake). Unlike Harvard Square, which my brother and I have both traversed a number of times, this was a new place for us, and I was glad our trip took us down a new path and helped us discover new things about the city of our youth.

---

references, but even if you took half of my estimate, you'd need more time then even the longest of lifespans to complete this task. Admittedly you could probably go faster then we did, but even then you're clocking in at just around a lifetime, and unless you finish this book (*Infinite Jest*, not this wee tome, but thanks) as a baby then you're already behind the curve, unless you're the *Infinite Atlas* webmaster or Wallace, himself, if you believe in that infinite time loop idea I mentioned earlier (and that presupposes he would even do such a thing, which means you're now wading into conjectural, multi-verse territory and ratcheting up the statistical improbability and oh my head is hurting).

There's a passage in *The Little Prince* about how one of the best things in life is walking down a side street and discovering a new world you never knew was there. I go back to Boston now, the closest city to where I grew up, go to New York, go on day-trips in my adopted city of Washington, D.C., and am always finding new worlds mostly by accident, although you can get caught up in the routine of life sometimes and forget about them, forget they even could be out there. It's not that the West Village, Cambridge, or MIT were places I didn't know were there, but they take on a new meaning when your body and soul stride to and fro in their immediate environs, in worlds of brick and mortar and thoughts and memories, the ghosts still walking along with us, in this strange and beautiful land of the living, bringing night too soon and a tall, cold one at the end of the day not soon enough.

*

If you ever go to Automatic Slim's you may notice a few candles burning on the bar top and a few photos of classic rockers hung above the bottles of booze against pale, egg-white painted walls. Or you may look outside, under the neon red sign bearing its name, as a bygone song plays out amidst the room, amidst maybe just you and the bartender, as you look outside and swear to God you see a burly man trudging down the street, shoulders hunched, brow furrowed, deep in thought and another world everlasting, until you realize it's just a shadow after all, or nothing, really.

Credits

First and foremost I want to thank my family, it's the truest of clichés to say I wouldn't be here without the love and support of them all. Mom for nearly going through the roof with excitement when I brought home my first high school newspaper article. Dad for helping me in my early battles with commas, and having <u>Leprechaun</u> marathons in Vermont. Shauna for the time we had Thai takeout and watched <u>Silver Linings Playbook</u>. And Steve, man, let's just say there wouldn't be a *PSH for President* without you, now get in the car!

Really everyone who has visited *BMC's Film Blog/PSH for President* these past five years, read something, left a comment, liked, disliked, loved, hated anything on the site, I can't thank you enough either. I would be remiss not to mention my Uncle Jeff, who has been an avid reader of the site over the years and provided plenty of encouragement along the way.

A special thanks goes to my friend, Devin Booth, who made this manuscript a hell of a lot better with his edits, and is just a good dude to boot, despite being a Seahawks fan.

The cavalcade of writers and artists whose work has compelled me to write everything here, in particular my mount Rushmore of tri-initialed artists- PSH, PTA, DFW, BKV- and Chuck Klosterman, as well as The Verve for "Bittersweet Symphony" and Oasis for "Don't Look Back in Anger."

About the Author

Brian Callahan is the writer of *BMC's Film Blog* (www.bmclassahan.tumblr.com), which will never be compared with the work of Roger Ebert. Despite messing up Battle of the Five Armies references and convulsing during the last Indiana Jones movie, his work has appeared on *TheOneRing.Net* and *The Wolf Review*. He was going to play an orc in The Lord of the Rings, but made an untimely joke about Peter Jackson having hairy hobbit feet, ending his career as an extra and ensuring he could never return to New Zealand. This is his first book[66]. He can be reached at bcallahan4815162342@gmail.com.

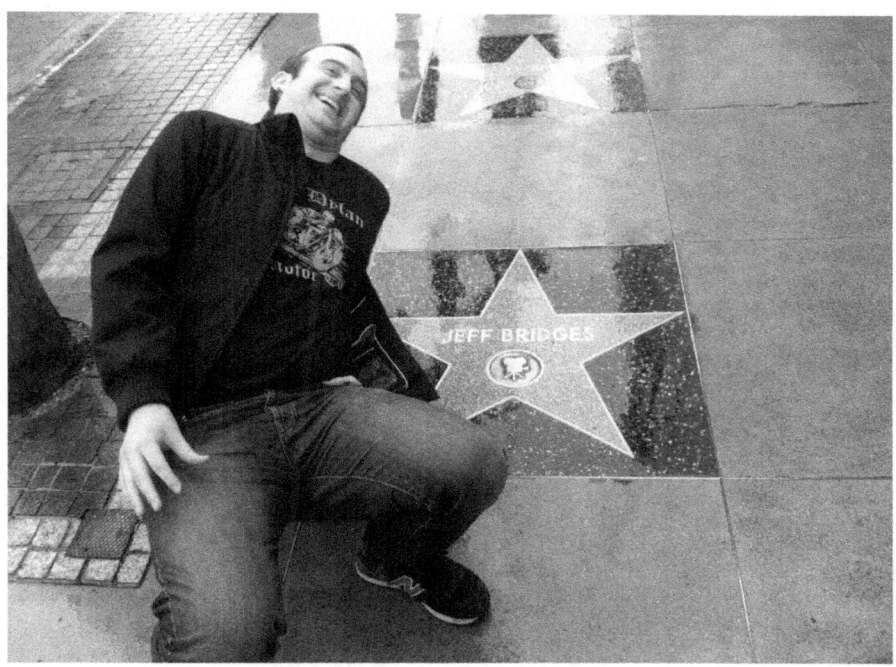

"The dude is not in, leave a message."

---

[66] And after all the lawsuits for defamation, probably his last.

www.ingramcontent.com/pod-product-compliance
Lightning Source LLC
Chambersburg PA
CBHW070044210526
45170CB00012B/581